ENDORSED BY

CAMBRIDGE
International Examinations

Cambridge
IGCSE®

English
as a second language

John Reynolds

HODDER
EDUCATION
AN HACHETTE UK COMPANY

® IGCSE is the registered trademark of Cambridge International Examinations

All the questions, example answers and comments that appear in this book and CD were written by the author.

Although every effort has been made to ensure that website addresses are correct at the time of going to press, Hodder Education cannot be held responsible for the content of any website mentioned in this book. It is sometimes possible to find a relocated web page by typing in the address of the home page for a website in the URL window of your browser.

Hachette UK's policy is to use papers that are natural, renewable and recyclable products and made from wood grown in sustainable forests. The logging and manufacturing processes are expected to conform to the environmental regulations of the country of origin.

Orders: please contact Bookpoint Ltd, 130 Milton Park, Abingdon, Oxon OX14 4SB. Telephone: (44) 01235 827720. Fax: (44) 01235 400401. Lines are open 9.00–5.00, Monday to Saturday, with a 24-hour message answering service. Visit our website at www.hoddereducation.com.

© John Reynolds 2014

First published in 2014

by Hodder Education,

an Hachette UK Company,

338 Euston Road

London NW1 3BH

Impression number	5	4	3	2	
Year		2018	2017	2016	2015	2014

Cover photo © Joseph Weber/istockphoto.com

Illustrations by Integra Software Services

Typeset in 11/13 ITC Galliard Roman by Integra Software Services Pvt. Ltd, Pondicherry, India

Printed in Dubai

A catalogue record for this title is available from the British Library

ISBN 978 1444 19162 2

Contents

Introduction

Cambridge IGCSE® Second Language English is an internationally recognised examination which assesses your ability to express yourself in English, both in writing and in speaking. It also tests your understanding of a range of texts written in English and how well you are able to listen to and understand someone who speaks to you in English. As the title of the syllabus indicates, the examination is designed for students whose native language is something other than English and it is offered at both Core and Extended levels. Your teachers will advise you as to which level of examination is more suitable for your present stage of development in using English. The different chapters in this book and the associated practice tasks will provide practice for both levels and all the types of task that you will find in the examination papers.

The exercises throughout this book are intended to provide practice for both Core and Extended candidates. However, a few exercises intentionally go beyond the specific requirements of the Cambridge IGCSE Second Language examination papers to allow teachers the opportunity stretch students who are capable of answering more challenging tasks. Such questions are indicated with the symbol ★.

● Your course

An IGCSE Second Language English examination, such as that offered by Cambridge, consists of six components, of which every candidate will be entered for three. Details of these are given below.

Component 1

Component 1 is the externally-examined Core written paper testing reading and writing skills.

- The Core paper allows the award of grades C–G and lasts for 1 hour 30 minutes. It consists of seven different tasks, testing both reading and writing. There will be a range of reading passages and questions will include items such as form-filling and brief report and account writing. There are 70 marks available for this paper.

Component 2

Component 2 is the externally-examined Extended written paper testing reading and writing skills.

- The Extended paper allows the award of grades A–E and lasts for 2 hours. As with the Core paper, there are seven different tasks testing a range of reading and writing skills, but the material is of a more demanding level – although it consists of similar types of writing. There are 90 marks available for this paper.

Component 3

Component 3 is the externally-examined Core listening test.

- This is the Core tier listening test and lasts for about 30–40 minutes. It involves candidates listening to a range of spoken (or recorded) passages of varied length, understanding of which is tested by a range of tasks including gap-filling, short-answer comprehension questions and multiple-choice questions. It is worth 30 marks and is externally marked.

Component 4

Component 4 is the externally-examined Extended listening test.

- This is the Extended tier listening test and lasts for about 45 minutes. It also involves candidates listening to a range of spoken (or recorded) passages of varied length, more demanding than those for the Core tier; understanding is tested by a range of tasks including gap-filling, short-answer comprehension questions and multiple-choice questions. It is worth 40 marks and is externally marked.

Component 5

- This is a speaking test and is not tiered. It lasts about 10–15 minutes and is worth 30 marks. It is internally marked in the Centre and then externally moderated.
- Candidates will engage in a short warm-up conversation with the teacher which is followed by a discussion on a given topic.

Component 6

- This is a coursework speaking assessment that is an alternative to Component 5. Candidates will complete three different tasks during their course which will be set and marked by their teacher and then externally moderated. It is also worth 30 marks.

① Becoming a better reader

Learning to read is one of the most important stages in anyone's development as it opens up so many opportunities. So many things in everyday life depend on your being able to read clearly. Here are a few examples.

- If you want to find out the latest news about your favourite film star or learn the details of the latest match played by the sports team you support, you pick up a newspaper and read what it has to say about these topics.

- If you are on a long train or plane journey it is almost certain that you will have a book, a magazine or an e-book to help you pass the time while you are travelling. Even if you are someone who 'doesn't read books' it is highly likely that you will have read the instructions or rules of the computer game that you are playing.

- Very often, you'll read something without even being aware that you are engaging in the reading process. For example, you might check the departures board at an airport or railway station or make sure that you put on the brakes of your bicycle as you approach the road sign that says 'Halt'. If you are unable to read, these necessary actions become either very difficult or impossible to achieve.

So, you understand how important a part reading plays in your life. Everybody who is using this textbook has mastered the art of reading to a greater or lesser extent. Why, then, you may ask yourself, is it necessary to have to read a book that tells you how to become a better reader – if you can read already, what is there to improve? And furthermore, why should you sit an examination which tests how well you can read something that is written on the question paper?

Well, the answer to this last question is that you should think very carefully about what you mean by 'reading'. Is it just a process whereby you decode words on a page and then speak them aloud or to yourself? Or is it something more complex than that? First let's look at the assessment objectives for reading.

● Assessment objectives

R1 identify and retrieve facts and details

R2 understand and select relevant information

R3 recognise and understand ideas, opinions and attitudes and the connections between related ideas

R4 understand what is implied but not actually written, for example gist, relationships, writer's purpose/intention, writer's feelings, situation or place.

● Reading with understanding

Let's consider reading something aloud. Think about listening to members of your class reading aloud from a textbook. Nearly all of them will have no difficulty in recognising and pronouncing the words written on the page. However, some will make those words sound more interesting than others. The ones who make the words sound interesting are the ones who read with 'expression'. They will emphasise certain words and phrases to suggest to the listeners that these are important points. If you don't put expression into your voice, what you read tends to become monotonous and the listeners soon become bored and lose interest in the subject matter.

If you can answer the question as to why one person's reading is more interesting than another's then you have understood a very important detail. To save you wondering too much, the answer to the question is that the interesting readers are those who have not just recognised the words but are attempting to gain a complete understanding of what the writer's intended meaning is. By doing this they are able to put much more expression into their reading.

Remember: reading without understanding is pointless. To do well, in so many aspects of life (including examinations in all subjects), it is essential that you think about what you are reading and don't move on to the next sentence until you are sure that you have as clear an understanding as you can of what is written on the sheet of paper or video screen in front of you.

The main aim of this section of this book is to help you to improve your understanding of the range of different types of text that you are likely to have to read as part of your Cambridge IGCSE Second Language English course, and in your life in general.

Comprehension

Comprehension is a word that means 'understanding' and questions in English examinations that test your understanding are known as 'comprehension questions'. They can take a variety of forms and can be based on a wide range of passages of varying difficulty. However, what you should keep clearly in mind is that the main purpose of all comprehension questions is to test how thoroughly you have understood what you have read – and that includes the wording of the question as well as the source material on which the question is based.

How should I read?

In order to read in the most efficient and effective way, especially when you are sitting an examination, it is important to become familiar with certain techniques that will help you to focus closely on gaining a clear understanding. The following points will help you to achieve this.

- Read the passage through from beginning to end, thinking carefully about the meaning of each sentence. Don't just ignore unfamiliar words, but try to work out what they might mean by looking at the rest of the sentence.
- Ask questions to yourself as you read. For example, 'What does this word suggest about the subject?' and 'Why has the writer included this particular detail?' and so on.
- Once you have read the passage through, think back over it and try to get clear in your own mind what the main points are. One effective way of doing this is to have a clear awareness of the topic sentences of each paragraph. Remember, a topic sentence is the sentence in any paragraph which contains the main idea of that paragraph. It is very often the first sentence but a writer may sometimes place it in another position for a particular effect.

- If you are reading something as part of an examination paper, you should also read the questions that have been set on the passage closely and make sure that you underline or highlight the key words so that you can focus clearly on exactly what is required in your answer.
- It will also help your understanding, particularly in an examination, if you can practise the skills of skimming and scanning.
  - **Skimming** means reading quickly through a passage in order to gain a clear, overall view of what it is about.
  - **Scanning** is a refinement of this approach, as it means you are reading in order to extract specific details which are relevant to the questions that you are required to answer.

Before we look more closely at how to apply these techniques, there is one other very important point to consider, and it is also one which is easy to overlook.

Identifying key words in a question

When answering comprehension exercises it is important to read through both the *passage* and the *questions* that are set on it. A clear understanding of exactly what the question requires will help you to focus on those parts of the passage in which the relevant points can be found.

When you are reading a question, you may find it useful to underline the **key words**. For example, look at this question based on the passage 'A Whale of a Time in Oz!' (pages 5–6).

> Read carefully the passage 'A Whale of a Time in Oz!' and then make notes of what it tells you about the behaviour of Southern Right Whales and why they were considered to be suitable for hunting.

From your skimming of this question, you will pick up that the passage is about Southern Right Whales. The key words to underline as part of your scanning process are the instruction *make notes* and then the specific details on which you are to focus: *behaviour* and *why they were considered to be suitable for hunting*.

For this question you are being asked to identify **facts** about the whales and about why they were hunted. You should, therefore, include only facts in your answer and not **opinions** expressed by the writer. Having a clear understanding of this difference will make it easier to keep your answer clearly focused on the question.

The passage has been printed with a teacher's commentary at the side, pointing out key details that will help your understanding as you read.

With these points in mind, we will now look at the passage.

A Whale of a Time in Oz!

In search of the Southern Right Whale 'down under'

Helen Highwater

A Southern Right Whale and calf

The first few paragraphs set the scene. Although you will be taking the details in as useful background information, you will also be aware that the Southern Right Whale does not receive a mention until the third paragraph. If you are reading actively, you will immediately notice this and be alert for further information which is going to follow.

As you read through the third and fourth paragraphs, it is likely that you will be asking yourself questions such as 'What do these details tell us about the whales' behaviour?', 'What was it about their behaviour which made them so easy to hunt?', and so on.

Getting there wasn't easy. First there was a 500 kilometre flight from Adelaide on a tiny plane shaped like a toothpaste tube. Then once we'd landed we met up with Gary White, our expedition leader, and his jeep. 200 kilometres along the Eyre Highway we entered the treeless Nullarbor Plain, a semi-desert populated mainly by Aborigines.

Our destination was the head of the Great Australian Bight, where we were to spend two days watching whales. On the way Gary told us what we wanted to know:

'Sadly, over 25,000 whales had been killed before whaling ceased in 1930. By this time Southern Right Whales were virtually extinct. They were known as "Right" whales because they were right for hunting in small land-based boats. They came close inshore, floated when killed, and had thick blubber, which produced the valuable whale oil when it was boiled down. This meant that the poor whales were hunted down in vast numbers by money-making shipowners.'

'Right Whales feed on small creatures at or near the surface, gently swimming along with their mouths half open, allowing the sea water to flow in. The water is pushed back out with their tongues, leaving the food behind. Thankfully, they are now a protected species and numbers have risen to nearly 800.'

This was a dismal tale but it had a happy ending – the whales were now safe from murderous whale hunters.

As you move on through the passage, you will find that it alternates between giving facts about the whales' behaviour and details about the scenery, and the writer's personal response to seeing the whales as they frolic in the water. The details of the scenery and the writer's opinions may make the passage interesting but you should be skimming over them as they are not details specifically connected to the questions which you are asking yourself.

In general, the language in which the passage is written is not difficult to understand and can be read quite easily by an average student. The vocabulary, for the most part, does not consist of long and complicated words. However, in the last-but-one paragraph the writer uses some more complicated sentences.

Two hours before sunset we arrived at our destination. The crumbling limestone cliffs dropped sheer into the deep blue of the bay. It was August, the height of the whales' breeding season. Every three years the whales come from their home waters in the Antarctic to their Australian breeding grounds. Mature females weigh 80 tonnes. The females do not eat at all until they return to the Antarctic. By this time they will have lost 20 tonnes in weight.

As the sun began to set behind us we looked out, but saw . . . nothing. Then boom! Right in front of us the sea erupted as a huge whale burst from the surface, thrusting its body out of the water and smashing down with a noise like a cannon firing. Again and again it surged from the sea, a majestic and thrilling sight.

After a meal under the stars we talked some more. Gary told us that large numbers of female whales and their calves had been in the bay the previous week. The calves are six metres long at birth and they grow to three times that length.

'This was Nature at its finest, awesome and strangely moving.'

Our final day began early. We packed up our camp, walked to the cliff edge and were amazed! I counted 24 whales. Swimming parallel to the shore, very close in, was a long procession of mothers and their calves. They floated past on the surface. Some swam side by side, others lazily rolled over each other as they moved slowly along. They were enormous. As they expelled the air from their blow-holes, great spouts of misty waters shot upwards. This was Nature at its finest, awesome and strangely moving. We were silent watchers of a primeval, wonderful sight. How can people hunt such beautiful and truly amazing creatures?

All too soon we had to go. In October the whales would return home too, home to the Antarctic. We said little. We'd been stunned by the size of Australia, climbed Ayers Rock and followed the tourist trail. These would become distant memories, but our two days whale-watching would remain alive in our hearts for ever.

Here, both the sentence structures and the vocabulary are more complicated. It is a good idea to slow down your skim reading at this point and stop to consider exactly what the words mean. Do these sentences contain information relevant to the question? If they do, then you need to consider how best to put the information into your own words to show a reader that you have understood. (Lifting the sentences as they stand and transferring them directly into your answer will be a sure sign that you do **not** understand them!)

Even if your understanding of the vocabulary used in these sentences is not entirely secure, your awareness of what the question is actually requiring you to look for should convince you that these are references to the writer's feelings or opinions. They do not have a great deal to do with the whales themselves, apart from telling us how impressive they are, which is a point made elsewhere in the passage anyway. You can safely pass over them and continue to read the passage. It will not then take you long to finish, as the remaining sentences may be of general interest in helping us to understand the writer's feelings but are not relevant to the material for which you are searching.

As you can see from this example, **selection of details** in your reading is vitally important to working under examination conditions. You must have a clear idea of what you are looking for and then focus on finding it and ignore any comment or detail which is not relevant to the question. The more swiftly you can select the details that you actually need to answer the questions, the more time you will have for expressing your understanding of them as clearly as you can.

Now let us look at how to apply skimming and scanning to a series of short-answer comprehension questions. The passage that follows (on page 8) is about the early history of the Eiffel Tower, one of the most famous landmarks in Paris. Here is an example of examination questions that might be set on this passage.

Read carefully the passage 'The Eiffel Tower' and answer the following questions.

a) Why was the Eiffel Tower originally built?
b) What was its particular purpose?
c) What was the full name of the engineer in charge of the project?
d) What was the name of the engineer who actually designed the tower?
e) Which word in paragraph 6 tells you that the Eiffel Tower was not intended to be a permanent feature of Paris?
f) How high was the tower when it was completed?
g) How long was the tower originally intended to last before it was taken down?
h) Why did Eiffel become a rich man?
i) What evidence does the passage give to show that the Eiffel Tower was a very well-made structure?
j) Why was it finally decided to leave the tower in position?

You'll notice that nearly all of these questions ask you to select **factual details** from the passage. Once you've read the questions carefully, you will have a clear understanding of the details you should be looking for as you start **skimming** and **scanning** the text.

1 **Skimming the text.** You will notice that there is a **title** that makes clear what the subject of the passage is; there is also a **photograph** that helps you to gain a clear picture of the tower (and may also help to explain what is meant by the phrase 'triangulated sections'). The passage is written in **short paragraphs** and you should use these to break down your reading so that you can appreciate particular details.

2 **Scanning the text.** Once you have a clear understanding of the passage you can select details that are directly relevant to the questions you have been asked and ignore sections of the passage that are not related to these.

Now put these points into practice by trying to answer the questions before reading through the commentary which follows the passage.

The Eiffel Tower

130+ and still standing

The Eiffel Tower is one of the most famous structures in the world. It was named after Alexandre Eiffel, whose team of engineers designed it. It cost £260 000 to build in 1889 with most of the money being provided by Eiffel himself and the French state. The Eiffel Tower rises to a height of 985 feet and for over forty years it was the highest structure in the world.

The top may be reached by using lifts and stairs with the first platform being 189 feet, the second being 380 feet and the third at 906 feet above the ground. The structure is largely composed of triangulated sections and this allowed the engineers to build the tower so high.

It was originally looked upon as a temporary structure, built for the 1889 World's Fair. The World's Fair coincided with the centenary of the French Revolution.

The Eiffel Tower was the entrance arch to the World's Fair and it was one of a number of designs entered as part of a competition. Alexandre Gustave Eiffel's company won the competition and so the tower became known as the Eiffel Tower. However, it was Morris Koechlin, an employee of Eiffel, who designed the thousand foot structure.

Koechlin was a junior employee of the Eiffel Construction Business, which specialised in the designing and building of bridges and viaducts all over the world. One of his first jobs was to design the framework for the Statue of Liberty.

Later history

The original idea was for the tower to be dismantled after a twenty year period. However, it was so well built and engineered that it was decided to leave it in position. The various parts (of which there were thousands) were so well engineered that not even one had to be returned to workshops for alteration.

After the first year of opening so much money had been raised from people visiting the tower that the cost of construction was covered and Eiffel became rich.

Alexandre Gustave Eiffel conducted experiments on the tower such as using it as a giant pendulum, a pressure gauge, an instrument for measuring air resistance and atmospheric pressure. In 1898 it was discovered that the tower could also be used as a magnificent radio tower. Consequently the Eiffel Tower was saved.

The Eiffel Tower – the most famous landmark in Paris

Adapted from *www.technologystudent.com*

Skim, scan and select

Now that you've had a chance to think about this, we can look more closely at how to read the passage and questions in the most efficient and effective way in order to ensure that you have the best chance of answering all the questions correctly.

- **Skim the text.** Remember, this process should include both the **questions** and the **passage** about the Eiffel Tower itself. You will notice that all the questions begin with the words *why, what, which* and *how*. This suggests that these are what are known as **'closed' questions**, in other words, questions that require a definite factual answer taken from the passage as opposed to 'open-ended' questions that will expect you to draw inferences or conclusions from what is written. You should, therefore, focus your reading on looking for appropriate **facts**.
- You will notice that there is a **photograph** with a **caption** accompanying the text. This will help you to picture more clearly what is being described in the passage. The passage has a **title**, followed by a **smaller title** and about half way through there is a **sub-heading**. All of these features contain details that your eyes will take in easily as you skim/scan the text and help to give you a clear, overall view of what it is about. Remember, all of these features are helpful clues to your understanding of what you read and you should make use of them whenever they occur.
- Once you have read through both the questions and the passage, you should then **scan the text**. In particular you should be searching for details directly relevant to the questions that you are answering. You may find it helpful to underline or highlight relevant sections of the passage.
- Next, **select the precise detail(s) you intend to use** to answer each question. Before writing down your answer, however, check these details against the wording of the question. This will help to ensure that you have answered exactly what was written and not what you *thought* was asked for.
- Finally, **write your answers**. Remember, you should avoid anything that is not relevant and include only the precise details required by the question. If you can rephrase the points (without altering the facts) so that they are in your own words, you will make it clear that you have fully understood the answer.

Breaking down the questions and the text

As mentioned previously, the questions ask for **factual details** that are contained in the passage. The questions are straightforward and, in all cases, the answers you give will be either right or wrong. Don't be lulled into a sense of false security, however. The questions may be straightforward, but they will still trip up a careless reader. Here are some examples of the sort of things that might catch you out if you are not careful.

- Question a) asks *why* the tower was built – if you're not concentrating you could easily misread this and think that it is asking you to say *when* it was constructed.
- Question c) contains two possible traps for the careless reader. Firstly, the question asks for the name of the engineer 'in charge of the project' and not the name of the engineer who designed the tower. Secondly, it asks for this person's full name. An answer which simply puts 'Eiffel' would not gain the mark.
- Question e) is testing your understanding of vocabulary. It is important that you quote the exact word in your answer and not the phrase in which it occurs (unless you underline the actual word that answers the question). If you don't know which word it is, you should try to work it out from the meanings of the other words in the paragraph.

- The answer to question h) cannot be lifted directly from the passage. You need to explain in your own words exactly where the money came from that made Eiffel a rich man.
- Question j) can be answered by referring to the final paragraph. However, in order to pick out the correct answer it is important to keep the key word 'finally' in mind as you scan the text.
- One point that you should quickly notice as you do the first read through of the questions and text is that the questions do not refer to the whole passage. For example, the second and fifth paragraphs contain some interesting information about the tower and its designer, but none of this is required to answer any of the questions.
- You should also notice that the questions do not always follow the sequence of the text. For example, the answer to question f) comes before the answer to question a). It is, therefore, important to read the whole passage in order to gain **a clear overview** of its content.

As you can see from this example, it is extremely important to be able to select relevant details quickly and accurately when working under examination conditions. As you skim through the reading passages, you should always attempt to gain a clear understanding of their overall content and then focus on identifying the key words in the questions, so that you can then select the precise points that will provide your answers.

The examination papers will present you with a range of reading passages comprising mainly non-fiction factual reading material. Some passages will be similar in format to the one we have just looked at as an example, but in others the information may be presented differently, for example as an advertisement, a leaflet, a newspaper report and so on. We will consider the different types of reading you may be required to do and the different types of question that may be set to test your understanding of them in later chapters.

● Practise your active reading skills

Here are two more reading passages (on pages 11–13) on which to test your reading skills. Practise reading through them and see how easily you can grasp their meaning. You have not been given any questions to answer, but it may help you to gain a more complete understanding if you think about the sort of questions that might be asked about each passage as you read through it. In fact, once you feel confident that you have gained a complete understanding of the material, you and a partner could write your own questions and then swap them over to see how well you do!

The first passage is another straightforward piece of informative writing, giving information about an exhibition recently shown in the National Museum of Singapore and containing historical details about the ancient Roman town of Pompeii which was engulfed by a volcanic eruption.

This passage does not contain any sub-headings or pictures as an aid to understanding so, as you read through it, you should concentrate on trying to identify the main points of each paragraph to provide you with the main details.

Study tip

A useful tip when reading this type of writing is to assume that each new paragraph deals with an important new point. If you can identify what we call the topic sentence in each paragraph, you will have found a good 'hook' on which to hang your understanding. For example, in the second paragraph of this passage the opening sentence is clearly the topic sentence. It states the main point of the paragraph and then the following sentences develop this point.

Pompeii exhibition opens at the National Museum of Singapore

The National Museum of Singapore transports visitors back 2000 years in time to experience life and death in the ancient Roman Empire. A new exhibition, Pompeii: Life in a Roman Village 79 CE reveals daily life in a city steeped in legend and mystery.

Pompeii and its neighbouring cities were buried – and frozen in time – after the fateful eruption of Mt Vesuvius on 24 August 79 CE. After being forgotten for nearly 1700 years, the city was accidentally rediscovered by well-digging shepherds in 1748. Since then, its excavation has yielded extraordinary artifacts – from beds, lanterns, hairpins to an exquisitely preserved 15-foot-long garden fresco from the House of the Gold Bracelet – and provided a comprehensive portrait of the life of a city at the height of the Roman Empire.

Amazingly, archaeologists have also been able to piece together the final moments of the people of Pompeii. By pouring plaster into cavities in the volcanic ash left by the victims' bodies, archaeologists were able to create moulds of the final moments of life in this once-thriving seaport. The exhibition features more than 250 artifacts uncovered from beneath 30 feet of volcanic material in this once-cosmopolitan city. The exhibition brings these priceless artifacts, along with body casts of eight of the victims of Vesuvius' fury, to Singapore.

Many of the artifacts had never been on public display until 2007, including a stunning large-scale garden fresco, gold coins, jewellery, marble and bronze statuary, and other dazzling examples of ancient Rome's artistry and craftsmanship.

The exhibition takes visitors through an average day in Pompeii; visitors walk a Pompeian street complete with storefronts and ambient sound, see samples of food items carbonised by the eruption, explore a home and garden setting from Pompeii, and see how the people of Pompeii expressed their spirituality.

The showpieces of the exhibition are the body casts, made from the cavities left in the ash after the bodies of those buried decomposed. These figures are caught in their last moments, shielding their faces, clinging to each other. Even a dog impression was preserved.

Adapted from *Archaeology News Network, Art Daily*, 18 October 2010

Facts and opinions

It is important that you understand the distinction between facts and opinions. Facts are objective details which can be supported by evidence. Opinions are subjective views held by the writer and cannot, therefore, be proved as being either right or wrong. For example, 'The Eiffel Tower can be found in Paris' is a fact which can easily be proved; however, a statement such as, 'The Eiffel Tower is the most beautiful building in Paris' is an opinion, as it is only the view of the speaker and there is no evidence to prove that the Tower is more beautiful than any other building in the city.

Now read the second example of a piece of informative writing (on pages 12–13).

- Note, however, that the writer has also included some of his own thoughts and opinions and not just presented the readers with factual details, as in the article about the Eiffel Tower.
- It is important that when you are scanning the passage, you have a clear appreciation as to which questions require you to identify facts and which ask you to show an understanding of the writer's thoughts and opinions. Be careful not to confuse opinions with facts as you are reading.

Golconda Fort: Hyderabad's time machine

The Golconda Fort transports you into a time warp.

Legend has it

The stories surrounding this beautiful fort are many. If you like ancient tales, your best bet are the tourist guides who swarm the entrance. They are full of stories that are intriguing, magical and most probably both fanciful and true. But they are stories that will surely keep you entertained throughout your long climb up the fort.

Here's the true story. Golconda or 'Golla Konda' (shepherd's hill) is a 13th century fort, built by the Hindu Kakatiya kings. According to a legend, a shepherd boy came across an idol on the hill. This led to the construction of a mud fort by the then Kakatiya dynasty ruler of the kingdom around the site. In the 16th century, Golconda was the capital and fortress city of the Qutub Shahi kingdom, near Hyderabad. The city was home to one of the most powerful Muslim sultanates in the region and was the centre of a flourishing diamond trade.

The city and fortress, built on 400 ft high granite rock, has a number of royal apartments and halls, temples, mosques, magazines, stables, etc. inside. Visitors enter through the 'Fateh Darwaza' (Victory Gate) studded with giant iron spikes (to prevent elephants from battering it down).

But that's just the facts. Legends and myths have always surrounded this mystical fort. Madhu Votteri, a practising conservation architect and author of 'A Guide To The Heritage of Hyderabad', talks about a holy mad man who was believed to be the actual protector of the Fort. 'Legend has it that Majzoob (holy mad man) stayed next to the Fateh Darwaza and protected it. When Aurangazab was ready to conquer the fort, the presence of this mad man never allowed his troops to infiltrate the gateway. Only when another Yousuf Saab, who was a soldier in the Mughal army, made him move from there, was the fort conquered,' says Madhu.

Ancient engineering

In fact, anyone who has seen happy tourists, clapping away merrily at the Darwaza will know the story behind its brilliant acoustics, one of the many engineering marvels at Golkonda. A hand clap at a certain point at the entrance can be heard clearly at the 'Bala Hissar' pavilion, the highest point almost a kilometre away. This worked as a warning note to the royals in case of an attack. Many walls of the inner buildings literally have ears. Whisper in one corner of the hall, with its great bare stone walls and empty windows, and you can be heard distinctly in another. This once enabled people to petition the king in private without risk to his security but nowadays just provides great amusement to tourists.

The gods are smiling

Madhu reveals that the Golconda Fort was unique because it held a lot of religious value for both the Hindus and Muslims. 'The Sri Jagadamba Maha temple atop Golconda is as famous as the Fort itself. In fact there was much secularity during those times. Ibrahim Quli Qutub Shah was popular among subjects and was also highly respected by Hindus. The two mosques in Naya Qila are a sight to behold too. The mosque of Mustafa Khan has a unique roof in Mughal style, while the Mullah Khayali mosque has beautiful Persian script engraved on its stones,' she says. There is also a Hindu temple on the way up. Story has it that Ram Das, a revenue official jailed by Abul Hasan Tana Shah, for misusing state funds, carved images of Rama, Lakshman and Hanuman on a rock surface in the cell.

Travelling tales

According to historians, a number of travellers came in and out of the fort, through the caravan route although not all could enter the fort immediately as it took them a lot of time and money to make their way through the gates of the fortress. 'So they would create make-shift settlements outside to live in,' says Madhu.

Also within the fort was a sarai (a caravan station for traders and travellers) as part of a Persian style garden built during the reign of Ibrahim Quli Qutub Shah. One story goes that during the reign of Abdullah Qutub Shah, he used to hear a woman's voice as she sang for travellers at the sarai, while he sat kilometres away at Golconda Fort. Her melodious voice was carried by the breeze, reaching the prince's ear at the fort.

Of gems and jewels

When the French traveller and jeweller Jean-Baptiste Tavernier reached Golconda in 1653, he found a fortress nearly two 'leagues in length' and requiring a large garrison for its defence. It was a town where the king kept his treasure. It was also an international jewellery bazaar, where traders from as far away as Arabia, Persia, Central Asia and Europe converged to barter for precious stones under the shade of its vast banyan trees. The Great Mughal Diamond, said by its owner, the Mughal Emperor Babur, to be 'equal in value to one day's food of all the people in the world' came from mines around Golconda, as did the Koh-i-Noor and dozens of other priceless gems. In fact, Marco Polo in his Book of Marvels is said to have spoken wonderingly of the Land of Golconda, identifying it as the mythical Valley of Diamonds in which, according to 'The Arabian Nights', Sindbad the Sailor had, centuries earlier, been cast down by a giant bird. If you reached down into the soil your hand would be filled with diamonds the size of eagle's eggs!

Adapted from 'Golconda Fort: Hyderabad's time machine', from the *Times of India*, 9 January 2013

Applying your reading skills

An examination such as Cambridge IGCSE Second Language English will test your ability both to read and understand material written in English and also to express yourself in that language in writing and speaking. In this and the following two chapters we will look more closely at the different ways in which your understanding may be tested and provide opportunity for you to engage in answering some practice exercises.

● The reading passages

The content of some of the reading passages on which you are tested and many of the questions set on these passages will be the same for both Core and Extended candidates. However, there will be some additional questions on the Extended paper which will require you to show an understanding of some of the ideas that are merely implied in the passage, rather than being directly stated by the writer. Questions such as these are referred to as **inferential** questions.

The Extended paper will also have an additional reading passage and questions to those contained in the Core paper. There are four texts to read for the Core paper (which lasts 1 hour and 30 minutes) and five for the Extended paper (which lasts for 2 hours).

Overall, the Cambridge IGCSE Second Language English Core tier reading questions will expect you to be able to do the following:

- understand straightforward texts such as notices, signs, timetables and advertisements and identify and retrieve simple facts and details contained in these texts
- read and understand a range of more complex texts (such as letters, brochures and fiction texts) and select and organise relevant information contained in them including ideas, opinions and attitudes expressed by the writer(s)
- show some understanding of what is implied by the writer(s) but not directly expressed in the text.

For the Extended tier reading questions you will be expected to do the following:

- read, understand, identify and select details, facts and important ideas contained in a range of texts including notices, signs, magazines and newspapers
- read and understand texts such as letters, brochures and more extended passages of imaginative writing and select and organise appropriate information and details contained in them
- identify and understand opinions, ideas and attitudes that are both explicit and implied in more extended texts and show an appreciation of the connections between these ideas and so on.

● The reading questions

Before we move on to look at how to approach some of the particular types of questions that will be set, it will help to summarise the key points which will ensure that you answer the reading questions as successfully as you can. Try to keep the following points in mind when you set about preparing to answer questions.

- You have plenty of time to read the passages carefully; don't rush into writing your answers until you have gained a clear understanding of what you have been asked to read.
- Remember that a careful reading and clear understanding of the questions is as important as reading the passages. This will help to ensure that you are in the best position to select those details that are relevant to the question you are answering.
- Read each passage through carefully from beginning to end in order to gain a general, overall understanding of it: it is important that you gain a sound overview of what it is about.
- Once you have achieved both an overview of the passage and a clear understanding of what the questions require, then look closely at the relevant sections of the passage on which the questions are based. It may help to underline or highlight key points in the text so that you can easily find them when writing your answers.
- The next step is to produce your written answers to the questions. Remember, it is important that what you write makes it clear that you have understood exactly what the question requires. A reader can judge your understanding only by what you have written, so don't leave out points which may seem obvious if they are relevant – if you do not include a point, you cannot be given credit for knowing it.
- Make sure all the details you include in your answers are relevant to the question, write your answers clearly and do not include irrelevant comments.
- Use your own words as far as possible to demonstrate your understanding. If you are asked to explain the meaning of a word such as 'exciting' remember that an answer which says 'something that makes you feel excited' cannot be rewarded as you need to use a word such as 'thrilling' to show your understanding.
- Remember: the more marks a question is worth, the more detailed your answer should be. You may have to refer to more than one part of the passage to provide a complete answer.

● Types of texts

The first types of passages that we are going to look at are those which are likely to be set for the earlier questions on both Core and Extended papers. Advertisements, brochures, leaflets, guides, reports, manuals and instructions will all be used as a basis for questions, although not all these types of texts will appear in any one question paper.

Owing to the nature and content of these types of writing it is likely that, for both tiers, the questions set on them will be quite straightforward and require you to identify factual details contained in the passage. They will almost certainly be of the short-answer type, rather than extended responses such as a summary. However, there may be questions on the Extended papers that will expect you to **interpret** some of the points that are not directly stated, for example by asking how the words used in an advertisement are aimed to appeal to a particular group of readers.

● How to approach short-answer comprehension questions

Short-answer questions are straightforward. They require brief, factual answers to show that you have understood a particular piece of information in the text. You should try to express your answers in your own words. Some questions will be worth more than one mark. Remember: the more marks there are available for a question, the more detailed and focused your answer should be. The way in which a question is worded will give you some indication of the approach you should take in your answer. Here are some examples.

- Questions which contain instructions such as 'Give two reasons' require straightforward retrieval of details from the passage.
- Questions which ask you to 'Explain' something, such as the writer's opinions, require you not only to say what the opinions are but also to make some comment about them in your own words.

The passage and questions that follow are examples of those that *might* be set for an examination. The comments which follow the questions contain details of points needed for satisfactory answers.

Read the leaflet 'Safe as Houses?' and then answer the questions that follow, before reading the comments for each question.

Safe as Houses?

Every year many children aged five and under are killed because of accidents in the home, and large numbers need hospital treatment. How can you make your child, grandchild or any young visitor safer in your home?

In the kitchen

The main types of injuries in the kitchen are burns and scalds, often caused by children pulling kettles full of boiling water over themselves or tipping up pans on the cooker. Other hazards include cups and teapots full of hot drinks, hot oven doors, and hot irons. Children can also be at risk from slippery kitchen floors and from household chemicals.

In the bathroom

Children can be scalded by bath water which is too hot, and they can also drown in the bath – even in only a few inches of water. Some children often like to investigate toilets, which can be unhygienic or even unsafe if some cleaning products have been used.

Slamming doors

When children are playing together it's very easy for hands or fingers to get caught in doors. Few of these injuries are serious but they're all very painful.

Falls down stairs

The under-twos are most at risk on the stairs because they try to crawl or walk up or down them before they're really ready to. Additional risks are caused by toys or other objects left on the stairs, loose carpet or poor lighting.

Falls from windows

As soon as a child is mobile, low windows, or windows with climbable objects in front of them, become a major hazard, especially on upper floors.

Fires and matches

Fire is the most common cause of accidental death in the home for children. Around half these deaths are thought to be due to children playing with matches.

Medicines and chemicals

Some houses may contain a selection of medicines and household chemicals which can be very dangerous if swallowed by small children.

Near the house

Children are also at risk near the house – particularly if they're unsupervised. Keep garages and sheds containing tools locked and take the same care with chemicals as you would in the house.

---

1 What are the main injuries that children can suffer in the kitchen?

This is a straightforward question requiring details from the second paragraph. The answer is 'burns and scalds' and can be found in the first line of the paragraph. These two words are all that is required for your answer. You might be tempted to add 'breaking bones from falling on a slippery floor' or 'poison from drinking household chemicals' but if you've read through all the questions first (as you have been advised to do), you will realise that these points answer a later question and aren't required here.

> 2 In what other ways can children be injured in the kitchen?

As mentioned on page 18, this is the question where you can answer with the points about slippery floors and household chemicals.

> 3 Give three items found in kitchens that can cause injury to young children.

This is another straightforward question and you have a choice of items to name. The answer would be any three from: (boiling) kettles, pans (on the cooker), cups and teapots (containing hot drinks), (hot) oven doors and (hot) irons. Notice that the question only asks for the items and not how they can cause injuries, although it would help to give a clear indication that you have understood the passage by pointing out that the kettles contain boiling water, the oven doors are hot and so on.

> 4 Which piece of information about the risk of young children drowning in the bath might some people find surprising?

This is a slightly more inferential question as the answer is not directly stated. However, if you read the relevant paragraph carefully you will realise that the answer is indicated by the use of the dash before the phrase 'even in only a few inches of water'. This piece of punctuation draws the attention of the reader to the information that follows and also draws your attention to the detail which is needed for a correct answer.

> 5 What two dangers to young children can be found in toilets?

The answer to this question is 'the danger of contracting diseases from germs' and 'the risk of poisoning from the cleaning products that may have been used'. You will note that the answer depends on your knowing that the word 'unhygienic' conveys the danger of contracting diseases through germs that breed in dirty places. It would not be correct just to write the word 'unhygienic' as this does not directly answer the question that asks for 'dangers'. Some people might be tempted to answer that one of the dangers might be falling into the toilet and drowning, based on the statement that children like to 'investigate toilets', but this is not specifically stated in the passage and there are two much more obvious answers.

> 6 Why are very young children at risk on the stairs?

It would not be enough to answer this question by saying 'because they might fall down the stairs'. The question clearly asks for a reason (Why?), so the answer would be 'because they try to crawl or walk on them before they are really ready'.

> 7 What precaution can you take to help prevent young children falling out of windows?

Again, this question requires you to make some inference. Although not directly stated in the passage, the answer is derived from the reference to 'climbable objects' so the answer would be 'to make sure that there is nothing for the children to climb on situated anywhere near a window'.

> 8 What else can cause dangers to children who are not being watched carefully by an adult?

This is a slightly more tricky question as it depends on your knowing the meaning of the word 'unsupervised' which is used in the paragraph called 'Near the house'. Once you have realised this then the answer is straightforward: '(sharp) tools and chemicals (kept in sheds)'.

> 9 What are the two most likely causes of danger to children under the age of five? What reasons can you give for your answer?

This question needs a little more thought as the answers are not clearly stated. One danger would be 'fire', as that paragraph mentions that it 'is the most common cause of accidental death in the home' (it may also help to bear in mind that no other question has referred to the 'Fire' paragraph, although you could not use this as a reason to answer the question!). The second cause would be kitchen objects that can cause scalds and burns as the passage refers to these as causing 'the main types of injuries'.

● Further practice in answering straightforward comprehension questions

Exercise 1

On page 21, you will find another leaflet, this time one advising the public about the problems that can arise from excessive noise. Read through it carefully and then answer all the questions that follow.

Noise

Noise is a form of pollution which can be merely irritating, or cause physical or emotional damage. For some people, the sound of music played very loudly is annoying, while others revel in it. Similarly, it may be enjoyable for some to drive a motor bike, while other people find the noise anti-social.

Long-term exposure to loud noise can bring about stress which has physical signs such as an increase in oxygen consumption and heart rate, possibly leading to effects on the heart and circulation. Tiredness, irritability and sleep disturbances may also occur.

The physical effects of noise on the ears can be serious. Prolonged, loud noise causes physical discomfort; it actually 'hurts the ears'. And if it is too loud or goes on for too long, it, at first, causes temporary hearing loss, then deafness, due to permanent damage to the delicate mechanism of the inner ear. Rock musicians performing in front of very powerful speakers frequently have permanent hearing damage.

Excessive noise can have a serious effect on health, and is associated with stress and anxiety. Very loud noise causes physical damage to the delicate structures in the ear and may result in deafness.

140 — DANGER TO UNPROTECTED EAR
130 — PAIN THRESHOLD
120
110
100
90
80
70
60
50
40
30
20
10
0

HEARING THRESHOLD

TYPICAL NOISE LEVELS DECIBELS

If used at too high a volume, MP3 players can cause severe hearing loss. Although the speakers are so tiny that they can fit inside the ear, the sound they produce is directed straight down the ear canal and can cause damage if the volume is turned up too high.

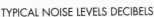

Don't underestimate the harmful effects of noise. It is the form of pollution which has the most immediate effect on people. It can cause severe stress.

From *The Environment and Health*, by Brian Ward, Franklin Watts, and *Wake Up to What You Can Do for the Environment*, DETR, 1989

1 What word in paragraph 1 tells you that noise damages our environment?
2 From paragraph 2 give three effects on people who have been exposed to noise for a long time.
3 What long-term physical effect of noise is mentioned in paragraph 3?
4 Which group of people is most prone to suffering this effect?
5 What is the reason given for this?

The next few questions refer to the illustrations and their captions.

6 Which word in the caption under the picture of the child resting on his bed tells you that it is wrong not to take the effects of noise seriously?
7 What reason is given as to why noise is such a great cause of stress?
8 Why do the speakers of MP3 players cause damage to the ears?
9 From the graph on the left of the page, what sound produces the loudest noise?
10 Which sound produces a sound of 85 decibels?
11 From the whole passage (including the pictures) state **four** ways in which we might unintentionally irritate other people with noise that we make.

Both the passage about safety in the home and the one on the effects of noise are examples of **leaflets** that have been produced in order to pass on information and advice to the general public. You will have noticed that they are presented in such a way as to make this information easy to understand at first reading. For this reason they use sub-headings, short paragraphs and graphics to help communicate their messages. Their content is almost entirely factual. As an additional task you could look again at both passages and try to work out exactly who the audience is at which they are aimed. For example, what is the likely age group of the readers? What are their social circumstances? And so on. Make sure you can give reasons, based on the content of the passages, for your conclusions. Once you have done this you could then consider how effective you think the passages are in communicating the information to their audience.

Exercise 2: Brochures

Another type of text on which the Cambridge IGCSE Second Language English examination questions might be set is a **brochure**. In some ways, brochures are similar to leaflets as they contain a certain amount of factual information and use photographs and other types of illustrations to support this. The overall appearance of a brochure is known as the **presentation**. However, the purpose of most brochures is not only to inform their readers about a particular place, for example, but also to attempt to persuade the readers to visit that place by creating an interest in it.

The example that follows is a brochure for a rather unusual theme park in India. Read through it carefully and then answer the questions that follow – there are a range of different tasks for you to attempt. (The brochure has been translated from its original language, so don't worry about the occasional expression which is not quite in Standard English!)

IT'S SNOW ALL THE WAY

It's indeed a wonder world in India, the indoor area filled with plenty of snow which is produced using state of the art technology, the snow is as natural as found in nature. It has largest snow area of 17 000 sq ft.

Once you enter, the huge snow filled area with −5 degrees Centigrade Oh! What a fun to have this chilling experience. Its thrilling environment with Polar Bears, penguins, Alpine Trees will leave you spellbound. What's more, you have the Igloo too.

The Cryozone of Snow World consisting of kids' snow play area, snow slide, snow merry-go-round, snow sculptures, snow basketball, Snow Mountain, snow volley ball, snow dancing, ice hotel etc. with snow fall in every session, that will take your breath away, yes, because it's snow all the way.

Protecting you from −5°C

Special warm jackets, gloves, socks and waterproof shoes will be provided.

Children below 2 feet (0.6 metres) in height are strictly not allowed.

Wearing warm clothes is compulsory for entering snow area.

Persons with heart & asthma problems and pregnant women must enter the Snow Area on doctor's advice only.

Things to do

1 Please deposit your cell phones at cell counter.

2 Please purchase camera/video camera permit ticket.

3 Entry starts half an hour before session time.

4   Collect shoe bags and deposit your footwear and collect token. No valuables to be kept in shoe bags.

5   Collect jackets, socks, gloves and shoes. While waiting, maintain queue.

6   Dress up and wait for the body to get acclimatised to lower temperature in lounge and later in air lock room.

7   Enter into snow area as per your scheduled session time.

8   Temperature in snow area will be 0 to –5 °C.

9   If you feel uncomfortable in chilling temperature you are allowed to go out to the exit lounge and re-enter within your session time.

10 After the session. Please hand over your jackets, gloves, shoes and socks at respective collection counters on exit side.

11 Return the token and collect your footwear bags.

Safety measures

- Please walk slowly and carefully in snow area – some places may be slippery.
- Please take care of your valuables, especially while removing jackets and gloves.
- Management is not responsible for any kind of loss or injury.
- All rides at visitors' risk.

Timings

SESSION	TIMINGS
1st	11:00a.m. to 12:00 noon
2nd	12:30p.m. to 01:30p.m.
3rd	02:00p.m. to 03:00p.m.
4th	03:30p.m. to 04:30p.m.
5th	05:00p.m. to 06:00p.m.
6th	06:30p.m. to 07:30p.m.
7th	08:00p.m. to 09:00p.m.

Prices

Snow World	ADULT (4 ft 6 inch/ 1.37 m & above)	CHILD (2 ft/0.6 m to 4 ft 6 inch/1.37 m)
	Rs 400/-	Rs 250/-
Snow World	College (above 10th class)	School (up to 10th class)
	Rs 275/-	Rs 225/-

NOTE:

1   FOR SCHOOL AND COLLEGE AUTHORISATION A LETTER IS REQUIRED FROM INSTITUTION.

2   MINIMUM 30 STUDENTS REQUIRED TO AVAIL SCHOOL AND COLLEGE PACKAGES.

Packages

PACKAGES	ADULT (4 ft 6 inch/1.37 m & above)	CHILD (2 ft/0.6 m to 4 ft 6 inch/1.37 m)	College	School
BLUE PACKAGE (Snow World + Rain Forest + Living Dead + Kalledo)	Rs 500/-	Rs 350/-	Rs 365/-	Rs 315/-
RED PACKAGE (Snow World + Rain Forest + Living Dead + indoor racing [4 Laps] + Kalledo)	Rs 680/-	Rs 530/-	---	---
DOUBLE OFFER (Ocean Park + Snow World)	Rs 600/-	Rs 400/-	Rs 400/-	Rs 350/-

Enquiry

SNOW WORLD: 040-65990167 / 68 / 69 / 70

9866699475

email: enquiry@snowworldindia.net

Special Packages for school, colleges, corporates & groups

Adapted from *www.snowworldindia.net*

1 State **three** things that you are told about the snow in Snow World India.
2 What is the temperature in Snow World?
3 From the information given in paragraphs 2 and 3, state **two** places in Snow World India where people might live.
4 Suggest **three** activities offered by Snow World India that would appeal to visitors. Say which age group (young children, teenagers or adults) would be most likely to enjoy each activity you mention.
5 State **four** items that must be worn by visitors to the snow area.
6 State **two** items that you must leave behind before you enter the snow area.
7 Are you allowed to take a camera with you into the snow area? How do you know?
8 What must you do before you finally enter the snow area?
9 In the 'Things to do' section, which word means 'to get used to the temperature conditions'?
10 What are you advised to do if you find that you are getting too cold?
11 What are you advised to do to avoid falling over in the snow?
12 How long does each session in the snow area last?
13 By looking at the language of the brochure and its presentation, explain how it sets out to persuade readers that Snow World India is both exciting and different.

Exercise 3

Your Year Group at school wishes to organise a visit to Snow World India. As a senior student you have been chosen to talk to parents to inform them about Snow World and also to encourage them to let their son/daughter take part in the visit. Make notes of what you will say in your talk under the following headings:

- What there is to do at Snow World (remember, there is more than just the snow area!).
- What visitors are required to do before they go and also while they are there.
- How long the visit may last and how much it will cost per person.
- Why students in your Year will enjoy the visit and why it could benefit their education.

Exercise 4: Advertisements

Another type of text that uses both words and pictures and which also intends to persuade readers to support its content is an **advertisement**. Advertisements usually make great use of presentational features in order to capture the reader's attention quickly and to communicate their message very clearly. One of the most common forms of advertisements are those seen in magazines and newspapers aimed at encouraging people to buy a particular product, ranging from washing powder to top of the range automobiles. Even though these advertisements may appear to be giving factual information about the advertised product, their main purpose is to persuade readers to buy it. They set out to persuade readers by appealing to their ambitions and other feelings by implying that the product will improve the readers' lifestyle.

Examination questions are sometimes set on this type of advertisement and will ask you to consider how the different features of the advertisement are intended to appeal to the reader. However, it is more likely that questions in an examination such as Cambridge IGCSE Second Language English will be based on a slightly different form of advertising – the public information advertisement. This is a text that has been created by either a government department or a charitable organisation with the intention of making the general public aware of a particular concern (for example, the need to conserve water or the plight of people made homeless by natural disasters such as earthquakes). It is also highly likely that such advertisements will also be aimed at encouraging the readers to contribute money towards supporting the cause that is advertised.

The following online advertisement is part of an online campaign run by a charity, Whale and Dolphin Conservation (WDC), to make people aware of the plight of these creatures and of ways in which individuals can help to protect them.

Read through the passage carefully and then answer the questions that follow. Some require longer and more developed answers than for questions that might be set for an examination, as they are intended to help you gain a better understanding of how the writers of the advertisement are trying to persuade their readers to support their campaign. You may find that it helps to talk over these questions either in your group or as a whole class discussion.

ADOPT A DOLPHIN NOW

And you will receive:

- A WDC adoption pack
- A certificate of adoption
- A WDC cotton bag
- Free magazine subscription
- Dolphin updates throughout the year

She's beautiful. She's intelligent. Don't let her die.

Every two minutes another dolphin like Kesslet suffers a slow, agonising death, accidentally trapped in fishing nets. Help end the suffering.

More than 300 000 dolphins die in fishing nets every year.

You can help save dolphins around the world by adopting a UK dolphin for just £4 a month. Adopt now.

WDC, Whale and Dolphin Conservation, is the leading global charity dedicated to the conservation and protection of whales and dolphins.

We defend these remarkable creatures against the many threats that they face through campaigns, lobbying, advising governments, conservation projects, field research and rescue.

Our vision is a world where every whale and dolphin is safe and free – including the dolphin you adopt.

Meet the dolphins

The dolphins each have their own personalities – click on the dolphin you'd like to adopt.

The dolphins of Scotland's Moray Firth are amazing but they face many threats. When you adopt a dolphin you will build a special link with an individual and help us to protect the whole population and give them a safer future.

Kesslet

Kesslet is a young mum who likes to hunt and play with her calf, Charlie. Kesslet is easy to spot because of her curved dorsal fin. She is friends with lots of the local dolphins like Rainbow and Moonlight and can be often seen travelling in groups of mums and youngsters.

Mischief

Mischief is a very friendly male dolphin who is always in a party mood! He is often seen in big groups leaping around with friends such as Rainbow and Sundance. Mischief is also a powerful hunter who can outrun even the biggest salmon. He is easily recognised by the big nick in his dorsal fin.

Sundance

Sundance was first spotted in 1990 when he was a tiny calf and now he's a big adult male bottlenose dolphin. Sundance is really sociable and he just loves to leap around with friends – especially Moonlight. We think he may be dad to Moonlight's baby.

Rainbow

Rainbow was first spotted way back in 1989 when she was just a youngster. She now has calves of her own including Raindrop who was born in 2005. She got her name because of her 'bright and colourful' character! She has a nick in the centre of her dorsal fin, which makes her easy to spot.

▶▶

Moonlight

Moonlight was first spotted in 1996 when she was very young. She now has calves of her own, including Mellow Yellow. She is easy to identify by the twin notches near the top of her dorsal fin. Moonlight loves to socialise with her best friend Rainbow. She's an amazing hunter – especially when she's in hot pursuit of lunch!

Spirit

Spirit was given her name due to her gentle and spirited nature. She has a calf called Sparkle, who was born in July 2007. She is often seen in the company of the other mums and their babies. Spirit has two very sharp nicks in her dorsal fin which make her easy to recognise.

Why adopt a dolphin?

'I can thoroughly recommend adopting a dolphin with WDC. It's a fantastic way to support their amazing work. Plus, you get to know an individual dolphin!' says Miranda Krestovinikoff, WDC Patron and BBC TV Presenter.

Oil and gas exploration and production, large marina development, pollution, fisheries and more are increasingly putting pressure on the dolphins and their home. By adopting a dolphin, you will build a special link with an individual and help us to protect the whole population. Extinction is forever – the Moray Firth dolphins cannot be replaced.

When you adopt a dolphin you will be helping to fund our work protecting dolphins around the world including:

- Essential research – the more we understand about the dolphins, the better we can protect them.
- Political campaigns to ensure effective laws are in place to protect the dolphins and give them a safer future.
- Equipment such as binoculars, cameras and acoustic recorders to help with our research.

Adapted from WDC (Whale and Dolphin Conservation)

1 What is this advertisement encouraging its readers to do?
2 State **three** things that are offered to readers to help persuade them to be involved in this activity.
3 How do you know that the dolphins referred to at the beginning of the advertisement (those who are trapped in fishing nets) are not killed on purpose?
4 In what ways does the WDC try to protect dolphins from the dangers they face?
5 What feature of her appearance makes Kesslet easy to identify?
6 Which two dolphins have a similar identification feature?
7 What fish would seem to be a favourite food of the dolphins?
8 What type of dolphin is Sundance?
9 Which dolphin is the mother of Sparkle and which is possibly the father of Mellow Yellow?
10 State **three** human activities that are a threat to the dolphins' existence.
11 Explain, using your own words, what is meant by 'Extinction is forever'.
12 Give **two** ways in which WDC will use the money that people donate to them.

 ## Questions requiring longer answers

1 Look closely at the first section of the advertisement (as far as the heading 'Meet the dolphins'). What effects are achieved by the use of short sentences and paragraphs? Consider also the use of facts and other information given in this section. How does this help in persuading people to support the campaign? In what ways do the use of bold type, the photograph and the language and content of the final two paragraphs of this section help to encourage the readers to support the charity?
2 Now read through the 'Meet the dolphins' section. What do you notice about the language used by the writers to describe the dolphins? In particular, you should consider the use of the second person pronoun 'you' to address the readers. What do you think the writers are trying to achieve by using words such as 'young mum', 'always in a party mood', 'just loves to leap around with his friends', 'with her best friend' and so on? Similarly, how do the descriptions of the qualities of the individual dolphins help to gain the support of the readers?
3 Finally, look closely at the final section of the advertisement (Why adopt a dolphin?). What effect do you think is achieved by the sub-heading being written as a question? The advertisement also includes a comment in direct speech made by a TV presenter; how does this help to persuade the readers to support the campaign? What do you think is the most important message that is conveyed in this final section?

● Further practice in reading factual/ informative texts

There are many different reasons for giving information and many different types of texts that are used for this purpose. Examinations testing your understanding of written English may use any of these, but it is likely that they will only use those which have a reasonable amount of written text rather than being entirely dependent on the use of pictures and other graphical features. It is also worth keeping in mind that in writing sections of the examination you may be required to write in a range of different forms and so it is important to be familiar with the styles of the various passages that we are using in this chapter in order to help you in your own writing.

Giving instructions

Some of the most simple and popular texts for giving instructions are the recipes used in cooking. It is important that these are as clear as possible so that those using them produce a dish that is as close as possible to that of the chef who originally wrote the recipe. However, the instructions in a recipe must also be sufficiently detailed to make sure that when you use them you don't overlook certain key ingredients or processes.

Read the recipe for 'Curried Pasta with Cauliflower and Chickpeas' and then answer the questions that follow.

Curried Pasta with Cauliflower and Chickpeas

I've always loved the offbeat combination of pasta and curry, and my family always liked it, too. The addition of chickpeas makes this a filling meal. This is a good dish to try out on older kids and teens open to new adventures at the dinner table. Serve with a fresh flatbread, a green vegetable (broccoli, green beans, or leafy greens) and a simple salad of tomatoes and cucumber.

Serves: 4 to 6

- 8 to 10 ounces pasta twists (cavatappi, or cellantani), rotini (spirals), or medium shells
- 1 tablespoon olive oil
- 1 medium onion, quartered and thinly sliced
- 2 cloves garlic, minced, optional
- 4 cups bite-sized cauliflower florets and stems
- 15- to 16-ounce can diced tomatoes (try fire-roasted)
- 2 teaspoons good-quality curry powder, more or less to taste
- One 16- to 20-ounce can chickpeas, drained and rinsed
- 1 cup frozen green peas
- $\frac{1}{2}$ cup dark raisins
- 2 tablespoons unbleached white flour
- 1 cup rice milk
- Salt and freshly ground pepper to taste

Cook the pasta in plenty of steadily boiling water until *al dente,* then drain.

Meanwhile, heat the oil in a wide skillet or stir-fry pan. Add the onion and garlic and sauté over medium heat until golden.

Add the cauliflower, tomatoes, and curry powder, plus $\frac{1}{2}$ cup water. Bring to a simmer, then cover and simmer gently for about 15 to 20 minutes, or until the cauliflower is just tender.

Stir in the chickpeas, raisins, and peas.

Dissolve the flour in just enough rice milk to make a smooth paste. Stir into the skillet with the remaining milk. Cook for 5 minutes longer, or until the liquid has thickened and everything is well heated.

In a large serving bowl, combine the cooked pasta with the cauliflower mixture. Season with salt and pepper and toss together. Serve at once.

Adapted from *The Vegetarian Family Cookbook* by Nava Atlas

1 Why does the author of the recipe say that adding chickpeas to this recipe is a good thing?
2 What group of people does the writer think would be a suitable group of people to try this recipe out on and why?
3 What types of pasta could be used in this recipe? Give a brief detail about each type you mention in your answer.
4 How many cooking utensils are needed to make this recipe?
5 According to the recipe, how long should it take to cook this meal?
6 Apart from following the cooking instructions, what else does the recipe suggest that you should do to complete the meal?
7 Is it important to include garlic in the meal? How do you know?
8 There are some technical terms used in this recipe. Find out the meanings of the following words and then explain what they mean: florets, unbleached, *al dente*, skillet, sauté, simmer, combine, toss together.
9 What does the writer mean by an 'offbeat combination' in the introduction to the recipe? Why is it likely to appeal to the people who are going to eat it?
10 Now that you've looked closely at this recipe, do you think that you would find it easy to follow or not? Give reasons for your answer.

Here is another piece of informative writing about food. This is not a recipe, however, but an extract from a website for young teenagers which offers advice and information about various popular fast foods, including details of which provide the healthiest options. The extract below is concerned simply with providing some background information – it may also help to explain why one of the most popular pizzas is known as the Margherita!

Read through the passage carefully and answer the questions that follow.

The history of the doughnut

Doughnuts have been around for centuries. Archaeologists found petrified ruins with burned fried cakes with holes in them. They were found in the Southwestern United States. No one knows how these Native Americans prepared their doughnut.

In the mid-19th century, the Dutch were credited with taking dough balls known as oily cakes or olykoeks and then frying them in cooking fat. The ones who really brought the oily cakes to America were the pilgrims. The doughnuts were made with apples and raisins in the centre. There was a problem though, when the oily cakes were pulled from the kettle the centre was hardly cooked. Inserting a filling that only needed to be warmed was the solution. That is how the hole appeared in the middle of the doughnut. That is the history of the doughnut.

The history of the hamburger

The hamburger was invented in New Haven, Connecticut in 1900. Louis Lassen, owner of Louis' Lunch had a customer who wanted lunch and the customer wanted it in a hurry. So the cook put the beef patty between two slices of bread. Louis' customers had a choice of tomatoes, onions, or cheese on the burgers. That is the short history of the burger.

The history of the pizza

The pizza, as the Italians called it, was created in 1889. Queen Margherita took an inspection tour of Italy. She found that many people were eating large pieces of bread. She was very curious about this

strange piece of bread that people were eating. She ordered her guards to bring her a piece of this bread. She absolutely loved it! She went back to her palace and ordered her chef to make the bread. Her chef Rafaelle made it special with tomato sauce and Mozarella cheese. It also had basil to represent the colours of the flag: red, white, and green. The queen absolutely loved this special bread and decided to call it pizza. That is the amazing history of the pizza.

From *www.thinkquest.org*

1 Which of the three items of food mentioned in the text was the first to be invented and which was the most recent?
2 According to the passage, who were the first people to cook doughnuts?
3 Why were doughnuts originally known as 'oily cakes'?
4 What was the original filling of a doughnut?
5 Why was it decided to put a hole in the middle of the doughnut?
6 What was the name of the restaurant in which the hamburger was invented?
7 According to the passage why was the hamburger invented?
8 Which feature of the pizza first interested Queen Margherita?
9 Explain fully the way in which the pizza was made to look like the Italian national flag.
10 What evidence can you find in the content of this passage and the language that it uses that the website from which it is taken is aimed at younger children?

Study tip

A useful tip when reading the type of writing that follows on page 33 is to assume that each new paragraph deals with an important new point. If you can identify what we call the **topic sentence** in each paragraph, you will have found a good 'hook' on which to hang your understanding. For example, in the third paragraph of the passage the opening sentence is clearly the topic sentence. It states the main point of the paragraph and then the following sentences develop this point. Spotting the topic sentences helps you to keep a tight control over your understanding of a writer's argument. Read through the passage and write down the topic sentence of each paragraph. You should find that this will help you to gain a clear understanding of the writer's main points.

Man is, pre-eminently, the animal who communicates, but until little more than a hundred years ago his thoughts could travel abroad no more swiftly than the sailing ship or the running horse.

The great change began when lightning itself became a messenger for mankind. At first, the electric telegraph was regarded as a superfluous novelty, but within a single lifetime engineers had spun a cocoon of copper wires around the world. In 1886 was laid the first successful Atlantic cable. From that moment, Europe and America were only seconds, and no longer days, apart. However, even when the telephone was invented in 1876 it was not possible to *speak* across the Atlantic; the early submarine cables could carry only telegraph messages. They were too sluggish to respond to the hundredfold-more-rapid vibrations of the human voice. Although a transatlantic telephone service was opened in 1927, it depended entirely on radio, which meant that even at the best of times conversations were liable to fadings and cracklings, and to eerie, Outer Space whistles and wails.

The first transatlantic telephone cable went into service in 1956. As a result of the vastly improved service, there was an immediate jump in the number of calls between Europe and America. More cables had to be laid – first across the Atlantic and later across the still wider expanses of the Pacific.

By the dawn of the Space Age, therefore, the problem of inter-continental telephone calls had been solved – but it had been solved so successfully that it had raised yet more problems. The cables could carry only a limited number of conversations, and it seemed unlikely that they could keep up with the rising demand. Moreover, just as the Victorian cables could not cope with the telephone, so the submarine cables of the 1950s were unable to deal with the latest miracle, television – and for very similar reasons. The electric signals involved in the transmission of TV pictures were a thousand times too complex to be handled by a cable. A new breakthrough was needed and the satellites provided it in the nick of time.

From *Voice Across the Sea*, by Arthur C. Clarke, Harper and Row, 1958

The next passage is taken from a website aimed at teenagers and is a report of a recent astronomical discovery. The questions that follow are intended both to test your understanding of the facts that it contains and also to help you to judge how successful it is in making clear the ideas it contains to its particular audience.

Goldilocks and the 3 planets

Space Scoop: Astronomy News for Kids

'Goldilocks and the Three Bears' is the tale of a picky little girl. Goldilocks doesn't like her porridge too sweet, like baby bear, or too salty, like daddy bear. She doesn't like her beds too soft or too hard. She likes things in the middle, like mummy bear: just right.

For this reason, we call the area around a star where the temperature is 'just right' for water to exist, the 'Goldilocks Zone'. These zones are not too cold, so that the water freezes, and not too hot, so that it boils away. These are just the right conditions for life to exist, too! Take a look at this image below; the blue stripe shows where the Goldilocks Zone lies in our Solar System. For hotter stars, the habitable zone lies further from the star, and for cooler stars, it is closer.

Now, astronomers have discovered a record-breaking planet system in the neighbourhood of our Sun. A nearby star called 'Gliese 667C' has at least six planets orbiting around it. Of these, three are sitting snugly in the Goldilocks Zone! Never before have there been this many planets where liquid water can exist orbiting the same star. If we can find this many 'Goldilocks' planets around every star, then the number of possibly life-bearing planets in our galaxy is much larger than we thought. And so is the possibility of finding alien life!

Cool fact: Three really is the magic number for Gliese 667C. Not only does it have three 'Goldilocks' planets orbiting it, but it is also part of a three-star system! If there is any life on one of its planets, the other two stars would appear in its sky similar to the full moon in ours – you can see them illustrated in this picture below!

This picture is an artist's impression of a newly discovered alien world orbiting around a star called Gliese 667C.

From *unawe.org*

The blue stripe in this illustration shows where the Goldilocks Zone lies in our own Solar System.

1 What is a 'solar system'?
2 What is meant by the 'Goldilocks Zone'? Explain using your own words as far as possible.
3 Why is the temperature band within the 'Goldilocks Zone' of a planet described as being 'just right'?
4 What is the difference between the 'Goldilocks Zone' relating to our sun and that in solar systems with hotter or colder suns?
5 What might be the most important physical feature of planets within the 'Goldilocks Zone'?
6 What fact, in particular, makes the solar system of Gliese 667C especially interesting to scientists?
7 What other exciting possibility is suggested by the discovery of the planets in the Gliese 667C solar system?
8 Why do you think the writer of this article refers to the story of Goldilocks in the opening paragraph?
9 How far do you think that the language used in this passage is successful in explaining the scientific details to the children at whom it is aimed? Can you find examples of words which might be difficult for them to understand?
10 Do you find the pictures included in the article to be helpful in understanding the content or not? Give reasons for your answer.

The final passages for this chapter (on pages 35–38) are two more examples of texts that give information, both of which are concerned with telecommunications. The first is an extract from a user manual for setting up a telephone answering machine. It is, of course, extremely important that instruction manuals of this kind contain only relevant and precise details as to what should be done, but, at the same time, they must cover every point exactly and in an order which can be clearly followed by the non-expert user. For this reason it is likely that they will make use of numbered or bullet points and simple illustrations. There is no place in this type of instructional writing for any other comments on the part of the writer.

Read through the instructions carefully and then answer the question that follows.

Setting up your answering machine

Recording the greeting

This answering machine has pre-recorded greetings. However, you can record your own greeting.

The greeting must be between two seconds and four minutes long.

You can record only one greeting, and it is used regardless of the answering mode ('normal' and 'announcement only' modes. See 'Selecting the answering mode'). Therefore, if you decide to change the mode, make sure that you record a new greeting to match the answering mode.

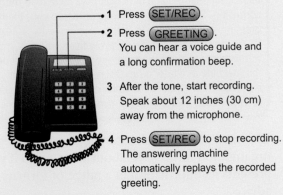

1 Press SET/REC.

2 Press GREETING.
You can hear a voice guide and a long confirmation beep.

3 After the tone, start recording. Speak about 12 inches (30 cm) away from the microphone.

4 Press SET/REC to stop recording. The answering machine automatically replays the recorded greeting.

▶▶

Notes

- If recording did not succeed, you will hear five short error beeps. Start over the procedure.
- If a call comes in while you are recording a greeting, recording is cancelled. Start over the procedure.
- If you hear five short error beeps while recording, the recording area may be full. In this case, erase unnecessary messages.

Tips

- If four minutes have passed in step 3, recording stops automatically.
- To record the greeting from a touch-tone phone, see 'Operating from an outside phone'.
- Even if a power interruption occurs, your own greeting is not erased.

Pre-recorded greeting

Normal mode:	'Hello, I'm unable to answer your call right now. Please leave your name, number and message after the tone.'
Announcement only mode:	'Hello, I'm unable to answer your call right now. Please call again, thank you.'

Tips

- If you wish to record your own 'announcement only' greeting, follow the above sequence after setting the AUDIBLE INDICATOR switch to ANN ONLY. Otherwise, the 'normal' greeting will be recorded.
- You have to change the message each time you change mode.

To check the greeting
Press **GREETING** to play back the greeting.

To change the greeting
Record a new greeting. The new greeting replaces the old one.

To erase the greeting
Press **ERASE** while playing back the greeting.
   The answering machine will answer a call with the pre-recorded greetings.

To go back to the factory pre-recorded greeting
Press **ERASE** while playing back the greeting.
   This will bring back the original greeting, but your own greeting is erased.

Imagine that your grandparents have just bought their first answering machine. They are not very technically-minded and although they have read the instructions, they find some of them rather confusing. They have, therefore, contacted you, their favourite grandchild, to help them record the greeting that they wish to use.

As they live some distance away from you, it is important that you do not just do this for them but that you instruct them on how this task should be done in case they need to re-programme the machine at a later date. Once you have read the instructions for yourself, write a detailed explanation of what needs to be done, in language that will be understood clearly by your grandparents. You should not simply copy out the instructions in the original manual.

This final passage is an example of an online guide issued by a government organisation in the UK, about what to do if your mobile phone is lost or stolen. It presents its information in a range of formats and provides both information and advice.

Read the text carefully and then answer the questions that follow.

Lost or stolen phone

Mobile phones now do so much more than simply make calls that many of us would be completely lost without them.

Unfortunately thousands of phones do go missing each year and many of these will have been stolen.

But if your phone does go missing you could be left with a much bigger headache than simply having to replace your handset.

Not only are many smartphones worth hundreds of pounds, but thieves can quickly rack up huge bills on stolen phones.

You may be liable for all charges run up on your phone before you have reported it lost or stolen to your provider. This is usually set out in the terms and conditions of your contract. Therefore, it's important you **contact your provider as soon as possible** to avoid facing high charges as a result of unauthorised use.

Protecting your phone

You should always treat your phone as carefully as you would your bank or credit cards. Make sure that you always take care when using your phone in public, and don't let it out of your possession.

Make sure you put a passcode on both your handset and SIM to make it more difficult for thieves to use.

There are a number of other steps you can take to keep your mobile safe and prevent against unintentional use:

- Make a record of your phone's IMEI number, as well as the make and model number. The IMEI is a unique 15-digit serial number which you will need to get the phone blocked. You can get your IMEI number by keying *#06# into your handset or by looking behind your phone battery.
- Consider barring calls to international and premium rate numbers (numbers which offer services you are charged for through your monthly phone bill or through credit on your mobile phone) to limit the usefulness of your phone to thieves.

▶▶

- Some mobile insurance policies may provide some cover for unauthorised use so it is worth checking the terms and conditions of your existing policy, or when considering a new policy.
- There are apps which can trace your phone if it is lost/stolen and can wipe details from it remotely – such as findmyiphone and findmyphone for Android.
- Register your phone with Immobilise, which is a database containing the details of millions of mobile phones and other property.

The National Mobile Phone Crime Unit is also a useful source of advice on how you can protect yourself from becoming a victim of phone crime.

What if your phone is stolen?

- Contact your provider as soon as possible. It can then bar your SIM to stop calls being made on your account. Your provider can also stop anyone else from using your phone by blocking its IMEI.
- Remember, if you have mobile phone insurance, you may be obliged to let them know within a certain time frame too.

To report your phone lost/stolen

Provider	Dialling from the UK	Dialling from Abroad
3	0843 373 3333	+44 7782 333 333
EE	07953 966 250	+44 7953 966 250
Orange	07973 100 150 (pay-monthly) 07973 100 450 (PAYG)	+44 7973 100 150 (pay-monthly) +44 7973 100 450 (PAYG)
O2	0844 8090 2020 (pay-monthly) 0844 8090 222 (PAYG)	+44 844 809 0200
T-Mobile	0845 412 5000	+44 79539 66150
Vodafone	08700 700191 (pay-monthly) 08700 776655 (PAYG)	+44 7836 191 191 (pay-monthly) +44 7836 191 919 (PAYG)
Tesco Mobile	0845 301 4455	+44 845 3014455
Virgin Mobile	0845 6000 789	+44 7953 967 967

From *www.ofcom.org.uk*

1 What reason does the passage give for saying that we would be lost without our mobile phones?
2 What **two** points make the theft of a phone such a serious problem?
3 What should you do as soon as you discover that your phone is missing?
4 What reasons are given in the passage as to why you should do this?
5 What **two** pieces of advice are given about how to keep your phone safe?
6 If you are the owner of a mobile phone, how else can you find advice about what to do if your phone is stolen from this article?
7 Explain, using your own words, what is meant by 'a unique 15-digit serial number'.
8 Why does the passage tell you to check carefully the details of your insurance policy?
9 Why should you contact
   a) the website findmyphone and
   b) Immobilise?
10 How can you stop anyone else from using your phone?

3 Reading more complex texts

Some questions on the Cambridge IGCSE Second Language English paper will be based on passages that are a little more complex than those we have already considered. In this chapter we will be looking at some examples of such passages.

The important thing to keep in mind is that the way you approach reading and answering the questions on these more complex passages is basically the same as that described in the previous chapter. In all cases, you should read the passage and the questions carefully and try to gain as complete an overview as you can of what the writer is saying. With slightly longer passages, it is a good idea to gain an understanding of the content of each paragraph (or group of related paragraphs) before moving on to the next. Don't forget to look for other clues that may help your understanding, such as pictures, diagrams, headings, sub-headings and so on.

The most probable reason for a passage to be more complex than those we have already considered is because it may contain a wider range of ideas. For example, instead of its being a straightforward informative or instructional piece of writing, it may also contain the writer's own thoughts and opinions and, as a result, be less straightforward. The type of passages that come under this heading are likely to be taken from newspaper or magazine articles and you will be able to practise reading and answering questions on some of these in the pages that follow.

● Note-making exercises

For your Cambridge IGCSE Second Language English examination, it is likely that the questions set on the more complex passages will require you to use them as a basis for a note-making exercise and, at the Extended level, to follow up on your note-making by writing a summary of the key points for a particular audience and purpose.

When you first look at a note-making task, it may seem to be very easy and not to require very much work as it is likely that the space allowed for you to make your notes will be quite small and you will be guided as to what you should write by a series of bullet points.

However, in order to be successful in attempting this type of task it is important that you focus your notes very precisely on exactly the requirements of the bullet points. This means, of course, that you must have a very clear understanding of the details that the bullet points are directing you towards, which means that you must read the terms mentioned in the question very carefully.

As well as understanding the requirements of the question, it is also necessary that you have a full understanding of the passage as a whole. You should then relate this to the overall purpose of the notes and/or summary that you are writing. By doing this you should ensure that you direct your response clearly towards the audience for whom you are writing and that you focus on the precise reasons as to why you are giving them this information. You may also need to select both facts and opinions from the passage – be careful that you don't confuse them; a fact is only a fact if its truth can be objectively proved.

So, as you can see, answering this type of question is a little more demanding than may at first appear and a successful response will require you to use your active reading skills to the full.

Reading practice

The passage that follows is taken from a newspaper article. It is a true account of a remarkable sea rescue of a lone sailor. You will see that it contains some graphical and layout features which are typical of this type of writing. When you practise reading this article, focus on trying to get a clear picture of what actually happened – the sequence of events – as in order to make the article more immediate and dramatic, the writer has not described the events in a strictly logical sequence. Remember, this is an opportunity to practise your reading skills – you are not required to answer any specific questions about the passage so it may help to work in pairs to gain as clear an understanding of the episode as you can.

'It's a miracle'

The thud of a fist and Briton is saved from cruel seas

Report by Ian Burrell

The rescue

It was the thud of a fist on the hull of Tony Bullimore's overturned yacht that told him he was not going to die.

The British yachtsman had spent four days and four nights in an air-pocket inside his capsized yacht, praying that he would be saved. 'I started shouting, "I'm coming, I'm coming",' he said. 'It took a few seconds to get from one end of the boat to the other. Then I took a few deep breaths and I dived out.'

It was the culmination of one of the most dramatic sea rescues of all time. Mr Bullimore had been stranded more than 1 500 miles from the Australian coast and 900 miles from Antarctica. The key to Tony Bullimore's incredible feat of endurance was an ability to remain calm and methodical in his thinking despite the most appalling circumstances.

The ordeal

Trapped in darkness, with freezing waters lapping at his feet and buffeted by 60 ft waves, he will have known only too well that he was more than 1 000 miles from the nearest land.

Faced with the danger of being dragged down with the boat, most people would have been tempted to try and jump clear.

Mr Bullimore's sense of calm, developed from years of solo yachting, taught him otherwise. He stayed with the yacht and quickly took stock of the few straws available for him to cling on to.

Yesterday he described the horrific conditions that he had endured.

'Two-thirds of the hull filled with water. There was a hole in the bottom of the hull, in fact really at the top, where one of the windows had come out. This caused water to be sucked in and out at a colossal rate, causing a kind of Niagara Falls, but upside down.

'This chap is not an ordinary person like you or me.'

'I had to find myself a spot as high up as possible and put nets around it so that I could crawl in there and lash myself in to get out of the water and to get away from everything.'

Dr Howard Oakley, of the Institute of Naval Medicine, said keeping a clear head and a sense of order were vital. Once he had decided to stay with the yacht, Mr Bullimore's priorities were to activate the distress beacon transmitter and to ensure he was getting enough air. Perched in a makeshift hammock, Mr Bullimore was alone with his thoughts, with nothing visible to focus on. This is the kind of situation that makes people motion sick.

Yet the discomfort of sea-sickness could not break Mr Bullimore's remarkable spirit.

'This chap is not an ordinary person, like you or me,' said a clinical psychologist, Eileen Kennedy.

'The kind of person who takes part in a solo yacht race welcomes challenge and risk.'

The survivor

The yachtsman said that during the 'horrific, traumatic experience' he was 'hanging on in there and believing something would happen and just fighting.'

'It was just determination, a little water, a little chocolate . . . hanging on in there.'

Through four days of darkness and solitude, he depended on 'sheer determination, a little water, a little chocolate' to sustain him.

But even Mr Bullimore was at his endurance limit.

'I only just made it. Because of weather conditions, I was deteriorating at a reasonable rate,' he said. 'When I knew that the rescue was actually going to happen, I felt ecstatic.'

Adapted from an article in the *Independent*, 1998

Example question

Before moving on to some practice exercises that you can answer yourself, we will look at an example of a newspaper article and the type of question that could be asked about it.

Read the question and passage carefully. As you read through you should also consider the notes at the side, which suggest ways in which a reader might think about the passage in order to gain a full understanding of it.

You are about to take part in a class debate in which you are speaking against the motion 'The technological inventions of the last twenty five years have been unquestionably of benefit to all citizens'. In particular you wish to question the value of using and owning mobile (or cell) phones.

Read the article written by John Naish (on pages 42–43) and use ideas from it to support these key points in your speech:

1 reasons why people think that we should all have mobile phones
2 reasons in favour of not having them
3 the main points I would use to persuade the audience to agree with me.

I refuse to use a mobile phone and I'm all the happier for it

By John Naish

My technology obsessed friend Richard rang my landline this week to make final arrangements for his birthday celebration: 'Have you still not got a mobile phone yet?' he asked, his voice dripping with disbelief.

No, I explained patiently (once again), I've not got a mobile and it's not a matter of 'still' or 'yet'.

I'm not making a stand against progress. I simply find life and work generally far easier without carrying what my 90-something aunt rather quaintly calls a 'portable telephone'.

According to conventional wisdom, as a journalist I should be permanently plugged in to all the newest versions of every available communications gadget, sifting all the latest data like a good little information drone 24 hours a day, seven days a week.

I did once own a mobile. It was back in 1999. All it ever brought me was hassle – a constant deluge of interruption from people calling for information they could have found out for themselves (and would have done so in pre-mobile days), or to tell me things that I didn't really need to know.

Oh good; that's helpful. There's a heading and it seems to give a good summary of the main ideas.

Nice picture but is there any way that I can use it? Most probably not, but it might help to convey the overall tone of the article.

If you don't use a mobile, you're treated as odd and maybe old fashioned – why should this be? There's a point for the first bullet here.

So, the writer's a journalist, but he obviously manages to do his job successfully without a phone.

This is a point I can use in the 'against' list.

I took the battery out, told the newspaper I then worked for that the phone was broken and said I would inform them when I'd returned to the airwaves. I never did.

Since then, over the years, people have developed varying responses to my mobile-less state. At first, they were condescending – why hadn't I caught on yet?

This reinforces the idea that phones are vital for people to manage their lives – it's the common view.

More recently, they have become disbelieving – how on earth do I manage?

This is another good 'against' point.

In the years since I dumped the mobile, the volume of interruption that people who do own one have experienced has become ever greater. It has rapidly taken up all the hours of the day that were once considered personal time when

The examples in the next paragraphs are good ideas to use for my argument in bullet 3.

you should be free of stressful work demands.

Sometimes, it seems as though there is no escape. But there is. It just requires a bit of self-discipline. I need to be near my landline during office hours when I'm working from home. Or, at least, I need to be near the landline at the times when colleagues or friends are likely to call.

I also need to be reliable so there will be no last-minute excuses or disappearances from me. And I need my internet connection to work so that I can access emails when I'm at my desk and read news websites and journals online.

However, during my mobile-free time, when I am off the electronic radar, I look after my

brain, letting it relax, think and recover from life in the information-overloaded 21st century.

At these times, you will find me in my garden or walking in the hills where I live, or riding a bike, or meditating, or simply reading a book.

I might even be having a long conversation with a friend in a coffee bar – if they're not checking their smartphone.

In truth, though, I am not entirely against having a mobile – but only if we could all use them sensibly and with consideration for others' mental space and time. But until we learn to use these toys responsibly, the personal stress and pressure are just too high a price for me to pay.

From the *Daily Mail*, 4 February 2013

Again (penultimate paragraph), two more good points to use – the second one can be developed to make the point about how using phones can be rude and anti-social.

The last paragraph sums up the whole argument against – mobiles are only useful if the users are in control of them and not slaves to the phone! Mobile phone users must learn to consider other people's feelings and personal freedom, despite the many benefits that these phones can offer.

Exercise 1

Here is another article taken from a newspaper. It differs from the previous passage in that it is mainly concerned with conveying newsworthy information rather than the writer's own opinions and attitudes.

Read through the article 'Women footballers bring new life to the beautiful game and score with Twitter' carefully and then complete the following task.

> You and many of your friends, both girls and boys, wish to set up a girls' football league in your local area. The authorities have said that before they commit money and resources to organising this they need to be convinced that there will be sufficient interest in the sport to make it worthwhile doing so.
>
> You have been asked to produce a report for the authorities in which you give reasons as to why a girls' football league would be successful in your area.
>
> Make notes for your report, based on Tracy McVeigh's article, under the following headings:
>
> ● evidence of the increased popularity of women's football
> ● how the social media have contributed to this
> ● the differences in attitudes of the public to men's and women's football
> ● why setting up a girls' football league would benefit your community.

Women footballers bring new life to the beautiful game and score with Twitter

Tracy McVeigh

After years of feeling underrated and overlooked by mainstream football pundits and press, women's football is coming into its own this season thanks to social media.

New research shows that the women's version of the game is now the third biggest team sport in the UK in terms of participation, behind only men's football and cricket.

Its previous lack of recognition is being overcome by fans turning to social networking to follow the sport. The second ever season of the Football Association's Women's Super League (WSL) kicks off on Sunday, and eight of England's top female footballers, one from each of the top clubs, will take the unprecedented step of wearing their success on their sleeve by displaying their Twitter account names on their kit.

The new semi-professional league, the top tier of women's football, was launched by the FA last year as a platform to drive forward the women's game and the association claims that it will be spending £3m on promotion in the first three years of the league.

Since the WSL launched, attendances have increased by more than 600%; viewing figures of live broadcast matches, at 450 000, are on a par with those of the men's Scottish Premier League, and the social media channels now attract more than 80 000 followers. It has transformed the player–fan relationship by making it a fully interactive league. Research commissioned for the FA by Sport England Active People ahead of the 2012 season shows that the low profile of women's football is what is driving fans to Twitter and Facebook for news. Fans are up to seven times as interactive as those of the men's game.

The Fifa women's world cup was the most tweeted-about event in the world in July 2011 with 7196 tweets per second at its peak. It remains seventh in the list of the most tweets per second, above the Uefa Champions League in 11th position.

But the findings show that while there are 12 times as many news articles with mentions of women's football per month, relative to the number of people who attend matches, men's football receives three times as many headlines, relative to the number of fans who attend.

'It is understandable in a way,' said England international and Arsenal Ladies midfielder Steph Houghton. 'It's difficult because the men's game is so big and attracts so much money and sponsorship and so it's always going to take priority.'

'But with digital media we can really forge ahead. We don't need to struggle to get a few lines in a newspaper, we can do it for ourselves; fans can interact with players and find out about fixtures and get really involved on match days – even if they are not at the game themselves.'

Houghton, 23, has been selected as the FA WSL digital ambassador for Arsenal Ladies this season. Each club in the league will pick one player who will wear their Twitter address.

'Twitter and Facebook have helped us massively, it's just transformed things over the past year,' Houghton said. 'It's really progressing the game. Our attendance figures have increased a lot. We're doing a lot of work in schools getting girls to play football, breaking down any taboos there might be, and we're seeing them get interested, and bring their families along where they have such a good match day experience that they're coming back.'

'I think that what's happening is that girls are enjoying playing. It's a lot more acceptable and now we have a Women's Super League with hugely dedicated female role models – really committed players who people can see are dedicated and training as hard if not harder than any male players – that's all progressing the sport. And with social media there's no holding women's football back.'

From the *Observer*, 7 April 2012

Exercise 2

Read carefully the following article, which describes the experience of a diver viewing the wreck of the *Titanic* as it rests on the seabed, then complete the following task.

> Imagine that you are the writer of the article. You have been invited to a local school to give a talk about your experience of discovering the *Titanic*. Make notes for your talk in which you include:
>
> - the appearance of the wreck of the *Titanic*
> - your thoughts and feelings as you explored it
> - your views as to whether it should be brought to the surface or left where it is.

Our second view of the *Titanic* was breathtaking. As we glided across the bottom, out of the darkness loomed the vertical knife-edge of the bow – the great ship towered above us and suddenly it seemed to be coming right at us, about to run our little submarine down. Gently we brought the sub closer until we could see the bow more clearly. It was buried more than sixty feet in bottom mud. Both anchors still hung in place.

Rivers of rust covered the side of the ship, some of it running the full length of the exposed vertical hull plating and pouring out over the bottom sediment where it formed great ponds as much as thirty to forty feet across. The blood of the great ship lay in pools on the ocean floor. Then, as we rose in slow motion up the ghostly wall of the port bow, our running lights reflected off the still unbroken glass of the portholes in a way that made me think of eyes gleaming in the dark. In places, the rust about them formed eyelashes, sometimes tears: as though the *Titanic* were weeping over her fate. Near the upper railing – still largely intact – reddish-brown stalactites of rust, the result of rust-eating bacteria, hung down as much as several feet, looking like long icicles. I subsequently dubbed them 'rusticles', a name which seems to have stuck.

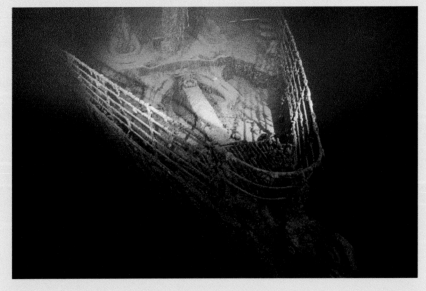

These rust features turned out to be very fragile. If touched by 'Alvin' (that was the name we called our sub), or dislodged by the thrust from one of our propellers, they disappeared in a cloud of smoke. And once the foamy crust had been knocked away, the steel beneath appeared almost perfectly preserved, only slightly pitted.

Carefully I counted the portholes aft from the anchor to locate the position where the ship's name should be, but I could see nothing.

Alvin rose farther, cleared the railing forward of No. 1 hatch, and we manoeuvred in over the *Titanic's* mighty forward deck. All at once I was forcibly struck by the sheer size of everything: giant bollards, the huge links of the anchor chains, and even bigger shiny bronze-topped capstans. Until now the ship for me had been somehow ghostly, distant, incorporeal. Now it was very close, very real.

I strained to get a look at the deck's wooden planking just four feet below us. Then my heart dropped. Gone was any hope of finding much *Titanic* woodwork intact, her beauty unblemished by the years. Except for a few fragments here and there, the wood was replaced by thousands upon thousands of small, white, hollow calcareous tubes one or two inches in length – the protective home of wood-boring molluscs.

I began to wonder whether the metal sub-deck would support us when Alvin made her first landing.

From *The Discovery of the Titanic*, Robert Ballard, Orion, 1995

Further practice exercises

The passages that follow are both written to give advice to tourists. The first is taken from an online guide to Norway and contains information about the weather and climate of the country. The information it contains is mainly factual and it is written in an appropriate **impersonal** or **objective tone**.

This passage also makes use of a graphical element; being able to show an understanding of how such features support the written content is a requirement of some questions in your Cambridge IGCSE Second Language English examination.

The next two passages (on pages 50–52) were written by visitors to the Efteling children's theme park in the Netherlands. They both describe the visitor's experiences at the park and also give advice and information to other families who may be considering visiting there in future.

When attempting to explain the function of the graphical features (such as a table or a graph) it is important that you keep clearly in mind both the purpose of the passage you are reading and the type of graphic that is supporting it. For example, the passage about weather in Norway, which is giving factual information to the readers, contains a map of the country and a table showing average daily temperatures for different towns on the map at different times of the year. It therefore clearly supports the information that has been written in the earlier part of the article and provides a summary of it which the reader can take in at a glance.

The Efteling articles are supported by photographs of two of the features that can be found in the park. You should consider whether the photographs are there simply to make the article as a whole more attractive in its appearance on the page, or whether they add to the content of the passage by providing information in a way which is difficult to convey in words.

Read the passages carefully and then answer the questions that follow.

Seasons, weather and climate in Norway

Because of the Gulf Stream, Norway has a friendlier climate than the latitude indicates. Check our weather report before you travel.

Weather forecast

Norway shares the same latitude as Alaska, Greenland and Siberia, but compared to these areas Norway has a pleasant climate.

Summer

Late June to early August is when the weather is warmest and the days are long and bright. Temperatures in July and August can reach **25 °C–30 °C**. At the same time there is hardly any humidity in the air.

Sea temperatures can reach 18 °C and higher, making swimming a popular pastime.

The warmest and most stable weather usually occurs on the eastern side of the southern mountains, including **the south coast between Mandal and Oslo**.

However, the summer weather can be wet and changeable, especially in Fjord Norway, Central and Northern Norway.

Autumn

In the autumn the temperature drops slowly through **September**, making for good berry and mushroom picking weather.

During autumn the land areas lose more heat than the sea, and eventually the coastal areas have the highest temperatures. In September the outer part of the Oslofjord usually has the highest temperatures. Later in the autumn, the warmest areas are usually found on the coast of Rogaland and Hordaland.

Winter

In winter much of Norway is usually transformed into a snow-clad paradise.

The lower inland areas, both in the southern and northern parts of Norway, can have very low mean temperatures in winter. Temperatures can reach **below −40 °C** in the inner areas of Finnmark, Troms, Central Norway and Eastern Norway, even if this does not happen each winter.

By contrast, the coastal areas have comparatively mild winters. However, gales, rain and clouds can be frequent and heavy.

Spring

May to mid-June is when the scenery in Norway is at its most spectacular, with trees and flowers waking to life, snow in the mountains and melt water swelling the waterfalls. Spring is the season when the temperature differences between the southern and northern part of the country are largest. This is also the time of year when daytime and night-time temperatures differ the most.

In early spring the coast of Western Norway usually has the highest mean temperatures, but in May the highest temperatures are usually found in the southern part of Eastern and Southern Norway.

The weather in spring can be very varied. There may be days when it is cold enough to snow, and days when it is warm enough to sit outside in the sunshine. Spring months can also be very windy.

Remember that the weather and temperatures can change quickly, especially in the mountains. So whether summer or winter, autumn or spring – prepare yourself for the wilderness and bring good footwear and warm clothes.

Average daytime temperatures

	Oslo	Bergen	Trondheim	Bodø	Tromsø
January	−2.3°C	2.7°C	−1.6°C	−1.3°C	−3.8°C
February	−1.3°C	3°C	−0.7°C	−0.9°C	−3.1°C
March	2.4°C	4.9°C	2.1°C	−1°C	−1°C
April	7.3°C	8°C	5.1°C	3.8°C	1.7°C
May	14°C	12.9°C	10.5°C	8.5°C	6.1°C
June	17.6°C	15.1°C	13.2°C	11.8°C	11°C
July	19.9°C	16.6°C	15.3°C	14.1°C	13.7°C
August	18.7°C	16.3°C	14.9°C	13.8°C	12.5°C
September	13.7°C	13.3°C	11.3°C	10.7°C	8.4°C
October	8.1°C	9.8°C	6.7°C	6°C	3.3°C
November	2.3°C	5.8°C	1.8°C	1.7°C	−1°C
December	−1.4°C	3.3°C	−1.1°C	−0.5°C	−3°C

From *www.visitnorway.com*

Imagine that you work for the Norwegian Tourist Board. You have received letters from two groups of people who are planning to visit your country. Both are asking for your advice as to when they should visit and which parts of the country would best suit their particular requirements.

Make notes for your replies to each group, as indicated below.

Group 1

This group consists of members of an outdoor activities club, based in Russia. They are very interested in skiing, walking in the mountains and related activities. You should give them information about:

- the best time(s) of year to make their visit
- the most suitable towns and areas of the country for them to visit
- the activities that they could take part in and any other information that might be of interest to them.

Group 2

This group consists of a family from Argentina who wish to visit Norway for a three-week holiday. The family is interested in seeing as much of the country as they can in the time available and consists of six people: mother, father, two teenage children and two grandparents, who are in their sixties but are both fit and active. You should give them information about:

- the best time(s) of year to make their visit
- the most suitable towns and areas of the country for them to visit
- the activities that they could take part in and any other information that might be of interest to them.

The two passages that follow describe visits made by families to Efteling Theme Park in the Netherlands. The first passage was written in 2013 and describes a visit made in the summer. The second passage was written several years earlier and describes a visit made in the winter. Read both passages carefully and then answer the question that follows.

Visit to Efteling Theme Park

The Fairy Tale tree

One of our fun-filled outings as a family with young kids has been to Efteling Theme Park, in the Netherlands. Efteling is one of the oldest theme parks in the world (rumour has it that the Disney Parks have been inspired by Efteling). It is a fantasy-based theme park and all rides and attractions are based on popular fairy tales, folklores, myths and legends. As you enter the parking lot the building with its pointed cones beckons you with promises and treats galore. Once you get inside, both children and adults are transported to a totally charming land of fairy-tale characters and interesting rides.

The park is based over an area of 160 acres (about 0.6 km²) and spread over a natural forest area with pine trees and many ponds and gardens which have been all used scenically to create an old world charm making it very different from a modern theme park. What I also want to say is there is a fair bit of walking to do. One can take prams for little ones or can even rent some push-cars for the older ones. You can also take a steam train from a quaint station which takes you around the park and its attractions.

Efteling started in 1952 as a theme park for children and then kept adding further features to become a park targeted at both adults and children. The entire park can be divided into 4 realms broadly speaking – Fairy, Travel, Adventure and Other Realm (names make more sense in Dutch, but presenting the English translations here) – based on the type of attractions.

If you go with young ones, you are most likely to do the Fairy Realm in detail, which is what we did in the half day we had there. Wander into the Fairy Tale Forest and encounter fairy-tale characters – Rapunzel lowering her hair, the dancing red shoes, the houses of Rumpelstiltskin, Snow White and the seven dwarfs, the Frog King, Sleeping Beauty, Long-Neck, etc. Most of these are houses which show the characters with all the props and the attention to detail is really commendable. The most compelling of the lot was the Fairy Tale Tree (Sprookjesboom).The tree tells all those gathered around it fairy tales and you can almost believe it's true as you see it moving its jaws. There are also these waste paper bins called Holle Bolle Gijs, based on the story of a very hungry boy, who keeps saying 'Paper here, paper here', basically meaning don't litter.

Litter bin

A must-see is Efteling Museum which also tells us about the history of the Park, a pity most of it is in Dutch. My personal favorite was the Diorama – a 3D miniature model of railways, houses, lives of the fairy-tale people. I also loved Villa Volta – a madhouse where you experience bizarre things. Raveleijn is a live animation show, based on a fantasy book for young children. There is a Steam Carousel which is popular, too.

I would say that it's impossible to do the entire park in one day, or half a day. There is an option to stay in the park in a hotel or outside in other hotels in Kaastheuvel, which gives you an option of starting early and exploring more. There are many options for food – also for vegetarians. If you are ever in the Netherlands or Belgium, do plan to visit this park.

Adapted from *Indian Moms Connect*, 2 January 2013

Cheesy ... but charming

by Sheryl Garratt

Soon after arriving at the Dutch theme park, Efteling, we were in a boat on a man-made waterway which is what you'd expect of a trip to Holland. Apart from the camels and the crocodiles ...

An hour later, we were floating again, this time in the air in open-fronted cable cars. The fairytale scenes before us on the Dream Flight were cheesy but charming, and beautifully done: the smells and temperature changed as we moved from one set to another; fairies perched in trees in a rainy wood full of goblins and trolls. My five-year-old son's favourite spot was the Fairytale Forest, featuring low-tech tableaux from various fairy stories.

These state-of-the-art rides are recent additions to a fairy tale-themed park that is almost 50 years old, set in the Brabant region near the Belgian border. Efteling's mature woods make it less artificial than most theme parks, with clever details like talking litter bins to keep little minds occupied and little legs walking. It's a great place to blow away the winter cobwebs.

We stayed in the Efteling Hotel, well suited for children. It has a generous play area with actors dressed as fairies and trolls. The family rooms were large and comfortable and the hotel has its own entrance to the park, allowing guests to get to some of the more popular rides before queues build up.

This is only the second year the park has opened during the winter months, as 'Winter' Efteling. Although the majority of the rollercoasters and white-knuckle rides are closed, and can be seen only from the carriages of a steam train which chugs around the park, there is plenty added on to compensate. There's a huge indoor skating rink, where small children glide along holding on to chairs and parents can have hot drinks in the 'après-ski' cafe. An indoor winter wonderland playground provides huge inflatables, snowball-throwing stalls and a snow slide that children can hurtle down on tyres.

On the crisp, clear winter days we were there, we were warmed up by frequent visits to reasonably priced stalls selling hot chocolate and delicious hot snacks (from doughnuts to French fries with mayonnaise). However, there is plenty to do undercover including the stomach-churning Bird Rok, an indoor rollercoaster, so even rain wouldn't have dampened our spirits. We spent more than an hour in a building housing a glorious 150-year-old steam carousel, an ornate miniature railway, a theatre where fountains danced to music and several refreshment areas.

Adapted from the *Observer*, 25 November 2001

You have been asked by the Publicity Department of Efteling Theme Park to produce a pamphlet aimed at families living outside of the Netherlands to encourage them to visit and to spend at least one day at the park.

Using the two passages on pages 50–52, make notes of what your article will contain. You should include the following information:

- a brief summary of the history of the park and an overall description of its main attractions
- the features of the park that would be of interest to different members of a family (for example adults, young children, teenagers)
- details of what the park has to offer at different times of the year and information about accommodation near the park.

● Information transfer

One of the tasks you will be required to do for your Cambridge IGCSE Second Language English examination is to read a piece of informative writing and then, to show that you have fully understood what it says, use the information contained in it to fill in a form designed for a specific purpose. This procedure is technically known as **information transfer**, as you are selecting information from one article and then adapting it to suit the requirements of a different form of writing.

Form-filling is likely to become an important part of your life as you grow older. Many adults find it an annoying and confusing procedure and claim that it is one of the things that they most hate doing. However, form-filling is not something that you can avoid and if you approach it with the same care and concentration as any other reading comprehension task you should soon discover that it is not as daunting a process as you might at first think.

The following points should be kept in mind when completing a form-filling exercise.

- It is essential that you read the questions on the form very carefully and ensure that you give the precise details required to answer them. Remember, in real life, the person who reads your form will have a great many others to read as well, most probably in a very short period of time. It is, therefore, very important that you provide the information required clearly, accurately and concisely. After all, one of the main reasons for filling in a form is as the first stage in an application for a job or for a place at a college or university – you don't want your future career prospects to be spoilt by your form being rejected as it has been incorrectly completed.

- Remember that you are expected to select details from whatever information you are using to answer precisely the questions on the form and that the person reading the form will be expecting answers to those questions and nothing else. For example, in an examination question, not all information contained in the scenario that is given to you is likely to be needed to complete the form. Always keep in mind the purpose for which the form is to be used and the role of the person (the audience) who will be reading it.

- Follow the instructions of the form exactly: if you are told to indicate an option by circling the correct one, then make sure that you obey this requirement. In an examination form-filling exercise, it is quite likely that failure to do so (for example by crossing out an incorrect option rather than circling the correct one) could mean that you are denied a mark that you could very easily have gained with a little more care. Similarly, if you are told to fill in a date in the Day Month Year order, ensure that you do this and not in any other format such as Month Day Year.

- A form-filling exercise may well require you to write one or two sentences at the end of the form to elaborate on the information you have given. This sentence will be marked for writing and you will lose marks if your sentence structure, spelling and punctuation contain errors, as well as if the information that you give is incorrect or incomplete.

- Remember, if a signature is required on the form it should be recognisably the same name as that of the person who is filling out the form. When under pressure of answering an exam question, it is very easy to sign your own name instead of that given in the task on the question paper!

- Finally, remember that forms are intended to provide information in such a way that it can easily and quickly be understood by the person reading it. It is important that you fill in the information neatly and legibly and make sure you use capital letters for sections of the form, if you are instructed to do so.

Exercise 1: Job application

Read the information below and then use it to answer the question that follows.

Maria Amaya is 16 years old. She lives at 37 Calle Ardiles in Buenos Aires. She has just completed her Cambridge IGCSE examinations and is looking for a temporary job for 6 weeks during her summer vacation. She hopes to gain good grades in her examinations and is planning to return to school to study maths and sciences in the 6th Form, and then to go to university with the intention of reading for a degree in physics.

Maria's family consists of her father, Juan, who is a journalist for a national newspaper; her mother, Constanza, a part-time teacher of English in a secondary school; a brother, Diego, aged 14, and a sister, Julietta, aged 6. Maria is an active sportsperson and is particularly keen on tennis, at which she has represented her school and local area. She also helps to coach the Under 12s at her tennis club. She is also a strong swimmer and holds advanced life-saving certificates. Apart from sporting activities, she is very keen on travelling to other countries and is a member of an outdoor activities youth group. She speaks English fluently.

While browsing the web looking for job possibilities, Maria saw the following advertisement.

Wanted: active and responsible young people

Aztec Holidays is looking for enthusiastic and hard-working young people to spend the summer working in their Children's Club in Cancun in the Yucatan peninsula in Mexico. The work will involve looking after children (aged 5–12 years) of guests at the resort and organising activities for them, using the facilities of the camp. There will be two 3-hour sessions each day, morning and afternoon. No formal qualifications are required as full training will be given before you commence work. Our club is run to the highest standards and we expect those who work there to be fully committed to protecting and entertaining the children for whom they are responsible. Accommodation and all meals will be provided at the resort free of charge and weekly pocket money will be paid to all employees.

If you are active, imaginative, responsible, enjoy working with children and would like to be part of our friendly team, complete the form below and return online without delay.

Maria decides this is exactly the job she has been looking for.

Imagine that you are Maria. Using the information on page 54, copy and complete the form printed below.

Aztec Holidays Cancun: Employee Application Form

Position applied for..

Applicant name..

Address..

....

....

....

Telephone contact number/email address...

....

Age on January 1st..

Dates available to work..

Name(s) of next of kin/contact numbers (in case of emergencies)..

....

....

Educational qualifications...

....

....

....

....

Sporting interests..

....

....

Languages spoken...

....

Experience of working with children...

....

....

In the space below, write two sentences. In one state why you consider that you are suitable for the position you have applied for and in the second sentence say what you can offer Aztec Holidays.

....

....

....

....

Exercise 2: Backstage tour

You are the Social Secretary of 'Outlook Youth', a youth group in your local area. One of your responsibilities is to arrange a variety of outings for the group members during the school holiday periods. Members of the group are aged 14–18 and comprise both girls and boys. During the last two years you have taken part in visits to historical buildings, a theme park and a zoo. Now, however, your members are interested in trying something a little more ambitious and it has been suggested that you arrange a visit to a large theatre in the capital city of your country in order both to watch a performance and to take a guided tour of the backstage area.

The theatre offers tailor-made tours to suit particular interests and this is what particularly appeals about this activity. They also offer to arrange overnight accommodation for visitors at a suitable hotel or hostel. As you will be travelling to the city by train and it will not be convenient to return on the same day as the visit, you would wish to make use of this offer. In total, 21 members of your group (including you) wish to take part in the visit (9 girls and 12 boys); the youngest is 14 and the oldest is 17. Three members of the group are vegetarians and one is confined to a wheelchair.

The leaflet that follows gives general information about what is available as part of the theatre tour and is followed by a task for you to complete.

Behind the Scenes

Backstage Tours

Explore the backstage life of the country's leading theatre.

The theatre is a working building, producing around 20 new productions every year. Play rehearsals, prop construction and costume making all happen on-site. No two tours are ever the same, so come and see what's happening behind the scenes today.

Tours run up to 6 times a day Monday to Friday, twice on Saturday and once on a Sunday.

Times

Monday–Friday: 10.15a.m., 10.30a.m., 12.15p.m., 12.30p.m., 5.15p.m., 5.30p.m.

Saturday: 10.30a.m. and 12.15p.m.

Sunday: 12.30p.m. (on days when the building is open)

Each tour lasts about 1hr 15mins. As the theatre is a working building, please note that starting times for Backstage Tours may vary and booking is advised.

- Visit unseen and backstage areas.
- Handle props from previous productions.
- Try out some costumes.

Costume tours

Selected weekdays, 10a.m.

See the craft and skill of the theatre's costume team, including the cutting room, dye shop and wig room. Each costume tour lasts approximately 2hrs.

In addition

Lunch and/or tea can be arranged in the theatre restaurant as part of the tour (at an additional cost per person).

If you wish the theatre to arrange overnight bed and breakfast accommodation at a nearby hotel or hostel for the night of your visit, please provide details of number of rooms required, etc.

Specially tailored backstage tours can be arranged both for individuals and groups up to 25 people. Prices are dependent on the nature of the tour required and a quote for the cost will be provided on receipt of the application form.

Use the information about your group and the Backstage Tours to copy and complete the following form as accurately as you can, in order to book the precise requirements needed for your group to attend a tour.

Behind the Scenes Tours: Booking Form

Name of organisation..

Contact name/position..

Address for communications...

....

....

....

Telephone contact number/email address..

....

Requested date/time of visit..

....

Number in party/age range of party..

....

Do you wish to book a tailor-made tour?*   Y/N

If YES, please indicate particular requirements in the spaces below:

Content of tour

....

....

....

....

....

Meals/refreshments requested

....

....

....

....

Overnight accommodation?*   Y/N

In order for us to find the most suitable accommodation for your party, please indicate maximum price per person per night...

Any other requirements (e.g. dietary, access arrangements, etc.).....................................

....

....

In the space below, write two sentences giving brief details about your party and what you most want to gain from your visit. You should write between 12–20 words for each sentence.

....

....

....

Please indicate by circling either Y or N

Exercises based on passages of imaginative writing

So far, nearly all the passages we have considered have been of non-fiction writing, aimed at providing information. To conclude this chapter, we will now consider two exercises based on extracts from longer works of **fiction**.

In order to answer the questions that have been set on these you should follow exactly the same approach as for the non-fiction passages. That is, you should read the passage carefully and try to gain as clear an overview as you can of its content. Next, make sure that you read and think about the questions and decide exactly what they are testing. As these are examples of **imaginative writing**, the questions will focus not just on details of what happened in the story and what people did, but are also likely to require you to give your thoughts and opinions about the behaviour and personalities of the characters in the story, and so on.

The first passage is an extract from the famous adventure story *Treasure Island*, written by Robert Louis Stevenson. The story tells of the adventures of a young boy, Jim Hawkins, and his adult companions as they go to the Caribbean to search for the legendary treasure of the pirate Captain Flint. At this stage in the story, Jim is the prisoner of another group of pirates, led by the villainous, one-legged Long John Silver, and the passage tells of the moment when they have finally discovered the hiding place of the treasure. (The passage has been slightly adapted from the original.)

Read the passage carefully and answer the questions that follow.

It was fine open walking here, upon the summit; our way lay a little down-hill, for, as I have said, the plateau tilted towards the west. The pine trees, great and small, grew wide apart; and even between the clumps of nutmeg and azalea, wide open spaces baked in the hot sunshine. Striking, as we did, pretty near north-west across the island, we drew, on the one hand, ever nearer under the shoulders of the Spy-glass Hill, and on the other, looked ever wider over that western bay of the island.

The first of the tall trees was reached, and by the bearings proved the wrong one. So with the second. The third rose nearly two hundred feet into the air above a clump of underwood – a giant of a vegetable, with a red column as

▶▶

big as a cottage, and a wide shadow around in which a company could have manoeuvred. It was conspicuous far to sea both on the east and west and might have been entered as a sailing mark upon the chart.

But it was not its size that now impressed my companions; it was the knowledge that seven hundred thousand pounds in gold lay somewhere buried below its spreading shadow. The thought of the money, as they drew nearer, swallowed up their previous terrors. Their eyes burned in their heads; their feet grew speedier and lighter; their whole soul was bound up in that fortune, the thoughts of the lifetime of extravagance and pleasure, that lay waiting there for each of them.

Silver hobbled, grunting, on his crutch; his nostrils stood out and quivered; he cursed like a madman when the flies settled on his hot and shiny countenance; he plucked furiously at the line that held me to him and from time to time turned his eyes upon me with a deadly look. Certainly he took no pains to hide his thoughts, and certainly I read them like print. In the immediate nearness of the gold, all else had been forgotten; I could not doubt that he hoped to seize upon the treasure, find and board the HISPANIOLA under cover of night, cut every honest throat about that island, and sail away as he had at first intended, laden with crimes and riches.

Shaken as I was with these alarms, it was hard for me to keep up with the rapid pace of the treasure-hunters. Now and again I stumbled, and it was then that Silver plucked so roughly at the rope and launched at me his murderous glances. Dick, who had dropped behind us and now brought up the rear, was babbling to himself both prayers and curses as his fever kept rising. This also added to my wretchedness, and to crown all, I was haunted by the thought of the tragedy that had once been acted on that plateau, when that ungodly buccaneer, Captain Flint, had there, with his own hand, cut down his six accomplices. This grove that was now so peaceful must then have rung with cries, I thought; and even with the thought I could believe I heard it ringing still.

We were now at the margin of the thicket.

The foremost of the pirates broke into a run.

And suddenly, not ten yards further, we beheld them stop. A low cry arose. Silver doubled his pace, digging away with the foot of his crutch like one possessed; and next moment he and I had come also to a dead halt.

Before us was a great excavation, not very recent, for the sides had fallen in and grass had sprouted on the bottom. In this were the shaft of a pick broken in two and the boards of several packing-cases strewn around. On one of these boards I saw, branded with a hot iron, the name WALRUS – the name of Flint's ship.

All was clear to probation. The treasure store had been found and rifled; the seven hundred thousand pounds were gone!

From Treasure Island by Robert Louis Stevenson

1 What feature of the landscape, mentioned in the first two paragraphs, marks where the treasure is buried?
2 Which one word used in the first paragraph tells you that the weather conditions on the island were very hot?
3 Why does the writer say that the third tree might have acted as 'a sailing mark on a chart'?
4 Describe in your own words the behaviour of the pirates as they approached to where the treasure was buried (paragraph 3).
5 Give the two words used by the writer in paragraph 3 which state how the pirates hoped to spend their lives after they had found the treasure.
6 What is the name of the ship on which Long John Silver and the other pirates had travelled?
7 What did Jim Hawkins, the narrator, think that Silver intended to do once they had found the treasure?
8 What caused Jim to stumble as the pirates raced towards the treasure? You should try to identify two reasons for this.
9 By referring closely to paragraph 5, explain, using your own words, what would seem to have happened when Captain Flint and his men buried the treasure.
10 What piece of evidence told the pirates that they were in the right place to find the treasure? What did they find and what had happened to the treasure?

The second passage is taken from the opening chapter of *Pollyanna*, written by Eleanor H. Porter, and tells of the preparations for the arrival of an orphaned girl, Pollyanna Whittier, at the house of her stern Aunt Polly, who is to be her guardian.

Read the passage carefully and answer the question that follows.

Miss Polly Harrington entered her kitchen a little hurriedly this June morning. Miss Polly did not usually make hurried movements; she specially prided herself on her repose of manner. But to-day she was hurrying – actually hurrying.

Nancy, washing dishes at the sink, looked up in surprise. Nancy had been working in Miss Polly's kitchen only two months, but already she knew that her mistress did not usually hurry.

'Nancy!'

'Yes, ma'am,' Nancy answered cheerfully, but she still continued wiping the pitcher in her hand.

'Nancy,' – Miss Polly's voice was very stern now – 'when I'm talking to you, I wish you to stop your work and listen to what I have to say.'

Nancy flushed miserably. She set the pitcher down at once, with the cloth still about it, thereby nearly tipping it over – which did not add to her composure.

'Yes, ma'am; I will, ma'am,' she stammered, righting the pitcher, and turning hastily. 'I was only keepin' on with my work 'cause you specially told me this mornin' ter hurry with my dishes, ye know.'

Her mistress frowned.

'That will do, Nancy. I did not ask for explanations. I asked for your attention.'

'Yes, ma'am,' Nancy stifled a sigh. She was wondering if ever in any way she could please this woman. Nancy had never 'worked out' before; but a sick mother suddenly widowed and left with three younger children besides

▶▶

Nancy herself, had forced the girl into doing something toward their support, and she had been so pleased when she found a place in the kitchen of the great house on the hill – Nancy had come from 'The Corners', six miles away, and she knew Miss Polly Harrington only as the mistress of the old Harrington homestead, and one of the wealthiest residents of the town. That was two months before. She knew Miss Polly now as a stern, severe-faced woman who frowned if a knife clattered to the floor, or if a door banged – but who never thought to smile even when knives and doors were still.

'When you've finished your morning work, Nancy,' Miss Polly was saying now, 'you may clear the little room at the head of the stairs in the attic, and make up the cot bed. Sweep the room and clean it, of course, after you clear out the trunks and boxes.'

'Yes, ma'am. And where shall I put the things, please, that I take out?'

'In the front attic,' Miss Polly hesitated, then went on: 'I suppose I may as well tell you now, Nancy. My niece, Miss Pollyanna Whittier, is coming to live with me. She is eleven years old, and will sleep in that room.'

'A little girl – coming here, Miss Harrington? Oh, won't that be nice!' cried Nancy, thinking of the sunshine her own little sisters made in the home at 'The Corners'.

'Nice? Well, that isn't exactly the word I should use,' rejoined Miss Polly, stiffly. 'However, I intend to make the best of it, of course. I am a good woman, I hope; and I know my duty.'

From *Pollyanna* by Eleanor H. Porter

Imagine that you are Nancy, Miss Polly Harrington's maid. It is the evening of the day described in the extract above and you are about to write a letter to your mother and sisters. Make notes for your letter in which you describe and give your thoughts about:

- Miss Polly Harrington and the house in which she lives
- your work in the house and your thoughts about what you have to do and how you are treated
- what happened when Pollyanna arrived and what you think about how she will cope living with Aunt Polly.

Once you have made your notes, you should then use them to write your letter. Begin the letter, 'My Dearest Mother …'

4 Reading and summarising

Writing summaries is one of the main tasks that you will be required to do in an examination. Although it involves writing, it is your **reading** skills that will really determine your success in the summary question. It is also important that you keep a clear head when attempting the task.

Summary writing is tested at both Core and Extended levels in your Cambridge IGCSE Second Language English examination (Components 1 and 2). The Core question will be linked to the note-making task that comes before it and will require you to write a summary of about 70 words, using the notes that you have made for the earlier task.

The summary question at Extended level will require you to read a separate piece of informative writing of about 300–350 words in length and to write a summary of the main points relating to a particular aspect of the passage in about 100–120 of your own words.

As you are no doubt aware, summary writing is a key skill which it is necessary to acquire, not just to be able to do well in your school work and examinations; it is also a skill that will be of great use to you in future life, for example as a student at university or in most of the full-time jobs you may have once you have finished your formal education. For this reason, although the advice and practice exercises contained in this chapter will certainly help you to prepare for your Cambridge IGCSE examination, they will also cover a wider range of approaches to meet the requirements of other school subjects and future responsibilities.

Types of summaries

Summaries come in different forms. You may have to:

- read one lengthy passage and summarise only the points contained in one or two paragraphs of it
- read one lengthy passage and summarise points related to a particular aspect or aspects of it which occur throughout the passage

No matter what form the question takes, the basic principles of summary writing remain the same. What is important is that you show **evidence** that you:

- have **understood** what you have read
- can **select the relevant information**
- can express the information **using your own words** and **in a shorter form** than in the original.

Remember that you will never be asked to summarise a passage unless it is possible to do so by using fewer words than were in the original!

Some practical guidelines

Whether you are taking Component 1 or Component 2, your summary writing can be improved if you keep the following points clearly in your mind. Summary writing needs good planning and cannot be rushed. Most examination questions will give a clear indication of the number of words that you should aim to write, for example: 'You should write 100–120 words', although sometimes this might be expressed as something like 'about a side of the examination answer booklet'. As you can see, the writing itself will not take very long; the most important part of the process is **deciding what to include** and **what should not be included** – that's why your active reading skills are essential.

It is important to organise your time efficiently when answering a summary question and, as part of your preparation for an examination, you should look closely at past papers and decide how long you have available to answer the question. Remember that this time allowance includes reading the original passage or passages, making notes of the relevant points and planning your answer. It is important that you spend most of the time available on these aspects of answering the question: if you have a clear understanding of what you are going to write for your final version, the actual writing of it will not take very long at all.

Once you have this basic approach clearly in mind, you can begin the task with confidence. Don't panic: remember, all the information you need to include will be in the original passage(s), so all you have to do is identify the really important points.

The following guidelines apply particularly to writing the type of summary based on aspects of a single, lengthy passage. Note-making is especially important – some examinations (such as Cambridge IGCSE Second Language English Paper 1) require you to write a list of main points which will be credited with marks before you write your final version of the summary.

Step 1: Read the question carefully

This is very important, as it is unlikely that you will be required to summarise the whole of the original passage(s). The wording of the question will direct you towards the points you should include. For example, the whole passage may be about everyday life in Japan, but you may be asked to summarise only what it tells you about going to school in that country. You must, therefore, keep the wording of the question clearly in mind when reading the passage(s).

Step 2: Read right through the passage(s) once

This will allow you to gain a good, overall understanding of what the material is about.

Step 3: Identify the information that is relevant

Refresh your memory of what the question asks you to do and then read through the passage(s) again very carefully. At this stage you should underline or highlight on the question paper all the information that is relevant to the question. You must be ruthless. Ignore anything that is not relevant, no matter how interesting you may find it. It may help if you give your summary a title.

Study tips

1 There may be some points in the original passage that are harder to find than others – the author may have **implied** them rather than stating them explicitly. Your final summary will be more successful if you are able to identify and include these implied points.
2 You can safely **ignore**: illustrations, quotations, long descriptions and strings of adjectives.

Step 4: Make notes in your own words

Now is the time to put pen to paper. You should make rough notes of the points you have identified. At this stage, it is not necessary to use your own words but it is important that each point is clearly identified so that the person reading your notes is absolutely clear what is being referred to. Remember, if you are taking the Cambridge IGCSE Core paper you will already have made your notes as the answer to a previous question.

Study tip

Check that you have made **each point only once**: it's an easy mistake to include three examples of the same point. The author of the original passage is allowed to repeat ideas; you don't have the space to do so.

Step 5: Count the main points

Once you have noted all the main points, count up how many you have identified. If you have identified 6–8 points and you are aiming to write a summary of about 120 words, then, as a rough guide, try to write about fifteen words for each point.

Study tip

One of the main mistakes in summary writing is to use up too many words writing the early points, so the summary becomes top-heavy and unbalanced. Remember that all points should be given equal weighting.

Step 6: Write the summary

Once you have written your notes, you should write them up as a piece of continuous prose, trying to keep your expression as concise as possible. If your notes are sufficiently detailed, this may only be a fine-tuning job.

Remember, at this stage, the use of your own words is important as this is the best way of showing that you have understood the passage(s). Try to:

- **paraphrase** (**rephrase**) parts of the text to which you refer
- use **synonyms** – words with the same meaning – instead of the exact words from the text.

This will make it very clear that you understand what you have read.

Study tip

An important word of warning – **do not include**:

- personal opinions
- extra information or explanations
- your own comments or opinions on the points made in the original text(s)
- quotations from the original passage(s).

The readers of your summary do not want to know your personal opinions about the topic; instead, they want to know how well you have understood the original author's viewpoint.

Step 7: Final check

Once you have written your summary, read it through to check that it makes sense. You may not have to count the number of words you have used, but if you know that, for example, you usually write about eight words per line, then a quick count up of the number of lines you have filled will give some indication of how many words you have written.

Study tip

Summary tasks require you to express your understanding concisely within a certain number of words. It's a good idea to focus your mind on this requirement when writing your answer. It is unlikely that a very long answer will gain the highest marks available for a question because you will not have shown your ability to select the key points and to stick to them. If you write considerably less than the suggested length it is most probable that you will penalise yourself (and reduce your score) because it is almost certain that you will have left out some of the important points.

● Style matters

In many summary questions, in addition to marks being awarded for the selection of the correct points, further marks may be available for written expression, as is the case with both Cambridge IGCSE Core and Extended papers. It is, therefore, important that you take care with the quality of your writing as well as the content, as these marks could have a significant influence on your overall grade. Remember, the copying of chunks of material directly from the passage will not score highly – this is because copying the text does not prove that you have understood it. It is important that what you write shows that you have understood the text and can interpret what you read.

Written expression: key points to remember

When writing your summary, you should remember the following points in order to achieve the highest marks for written expression.

- The best answers will be concisely expressed, well organised and clearly focused on the topic. They will show a good attempt to use your own words rather than rely on those of the writer of the original. Written expression will be generally accurate.
- Middle range answers will show understanding of the passage, but are likely to do so through selective lifting of language from the original. There will be an attempt to sequence the points in a logical order; there are likely to be some inaccuracies in written expression.
- The least successful answers will contain a large amount of language copied directly from the original, with the result that understanding of the key points is not clearly communicated. Frequent and serious errors of expression will also significantly obscure the communication of ideas.

Further advice

The bullet points below contain some important advice that should be followed very carefully.

- Concision of expression is something which typifies the very best summaries. This can be achieved by making sure that you focus clearly on only the points stated in the wording of the question.
- One way of doing this is to make sure that you don't include any irrelevant comments. For instance, a generalised introductory paragraph is not necessary and simply uses up words unnecessarily.
- Lifting (or quoting) whole phrases or sentences from the original will not give a clear indication that you have understood the text.
- A summary should be written using an objective, impersonal register; there is no need to comment or to write in the first person – even if that is the way in which the original has been written.

Example of a summary question

The passage that follows is taken from a magazine published in the UK and gives advice as to how to deal with difficult neighbours. You should keep in mind when reading it that the problems that arise, and the solutions suggested, apply to the UK only and may not be appropriate for dealing with troublesome neighbours in the country in which you live!

The example summary that follows the passage is a combination of the approach required for both Core and Extended Cambridge IGCSE Second Language English papers.

Here is the question set on the passage.

> Read the passage carefully and then
>
> a) Make notes about:
>   i) the problems caused by neighbours mentioned in the passage
>   ii) the advice given about how to deal with these problems.
> b) Write one or two paragraphs of 100–120 words in total, in which you describe the problems caused by some neighbours and explain how you should deal with them.

The passage has been annotated with the problems highlighted in yellow and the advice highlighted in pink. These points are then listed in note form at the end of the passage and are followed by an example of a written response to question b) based on the key points.

> **Note:** This passage is for example only as it is slightly longer than the sort of passage that will be set for your examination.

A clash with a neighbour can make life hell. And if things turn sour between you and your neighbour, you may not be able to get away from the problem – unless you move house. For this report, we take the disputes which people have most often with neighbours and explain how to deal with each of them.

Noise next door can drive you mad. It could come from building work or from non-stop, all-night parties. If you can't bear it any longer, contact the Environmental Health Department of your local council. You'll need to prove that the noise stops you from enjoying your property or that it is making you ill. You will need proof, so keep a diary.

Many house and car alarms seem to go off for no reason at any time of the day or night. If this is a problem, you can phone either the police or your local Environmental Health Officer. There is a new law which allows them to turn off a car alarm, and to enter premises to disconnect an alarm which keeps going off.

If your neighbours have the builders in, you may have to put up with drills and cement mixers. There is bound to be some disturbance; but if you cannot bear the noise, or it is taking place at night, then you can take them to court to make them stop work. This is called taking out an injunction.

The parking place right outside your house is not part of your property. You have no legal right to park there. However, you have a legal right to enter your driveway or garage. Some local councils now operate parking schemes for residents. If your neighbours are always parking so you can't get out, contact the Highways Department of your local council. It is in charge of traffic management and control. Call the police if you think your neighbour's parking habits are illegal.

If your neighbour fences off some of your land or starts growing plants in what you think is your garden then you have a problem. Arguments over land ownership are hard to solve. They can be sorted out in court but this could cost you a lot of money. You have to decide just how much time and money you are prepared to spend.

Many complaints are about neighbours' building extensions. People who wish to build extensions must have planning permission. The council must put up a notice at the site or write to all those who may be affected. You have 21 days to object to the proposal. Put your objection in writing to the local Planning Department and try to get other people to do so, too. We hope that the information above will be useful. Good luck!

Adapted from *Which?* magazine

Here are the key points set out as notes side by side in a table.

Problem	Advice
Noise: House/car alarms Building noise (especially at night)	Contact EHO; keep a diary Contact police or EHO Take out an injunction through the courts
Obstructive parking Illegal parking	Contact Highways Department Call the police
Neighbour fencing off your land	Go to court but this may be very expensive
Building extensions	Notification must be published. You have 21 days to object to the local Planning Department

Example summary

If you are disturbed by noise from your neighbour you keep a diary of when it occurs and report the matter to your Environmental Health Department; if the noise is at night, for example, from building work, you can take your neighbours to court and get a court order to make them stop. You should contact the Highways Department if a neighbour parks in such a way that you can't access your property or the police if their parking is illegal. If neighbours put up a fence that infringes on your property you can take them to court but this could be very expensive. Finally, if you are not happy with a neighbour's planned building extension, you can object to the local Planning Department within 21 days of the proposal being published.

● Practise summary writing

Here are some further passages for you to use to practise writing summaries. In all cases, you should read the passage and the question carefully, make notes in list form and then use the notes to write your final summary.

You will have seen and possibly made notes on some of the passages already as they were part of an exercise in an earlier chapter, but they are printed again here for your convenience.

Exercise 1

Read the following passage carefully and then write a summary of what it tells you about the building and design of the Channel Tunnel. (Note that the Channel Tunnel is also known as the Chunnel.)

The Channel Tunnel

By Jennifer Rosenberg

In 1984, the French and British agreed that a link across the English Channel would be mutually beneficial. However, both governments realised that although the project would create much needed jobs, neither country's government could fund such a massive project. Thus, they decided to hold a contest.

This contest invited companies to submit their plans to create a link across the English Channel. As part of the contest's requirements, the submitting company was to provide a plan to raise the needed funds to build the project, have the ability to operate the proposed Channel link once the project was completed, and the proposed link must be able to endure for at least 120 years.

Ten proposals were submitted, including various tunnels and bridges. Some of the proposals were so outlandish in design that they were easily dismissed; others would be so expensive that they were unlikely to ever be completed. The successful proposal planned for a tunnel made up of two, parallel railway tunnels that would be dug under the English Channel. Between these two railway tunnels would run a third, smaller tunnel that would be used for maintenance, including drainage pipes, communication cables, etc.

Some trains that would run through the Chunnel would carry passengers only. Other trains, known as 'shuttles', would be able to hold cars and trucks. This would enable personal vehicles to go through the Channel Tunnel without having individual drivers face such a long, underground drive. Also, large train terminals had to be built at Folkestone in Great Britain and Coquelles in France.

On 10 December 1993, the first test run was completed through the entire Channel Tunnel. After additional fine tuning, the Channel Tunnel officially opened on 6 May 1994.

Adapted from *About.com Guide*

Exercise 2

Read carefully the following article which describes how a man survived an attack by a black bear. Write a summary of what the passage tells you about:

- how the bear attacked and how the writer responded
- the writer's thoughts and feelings during this experience.

Bear Attack

A few years ago, I lived alone in a tiny log cabin in the wilderness of Alaska for a book I was writing. One day, I was bathing in the river after a day chopping wood for the cabin I was building. I was happily brushing my teeth when an unexpected movement caught my eye upstream. I pulled myself up on to a tree trunk to take a closer look. And my heart jumped into my mouth.

A huge black bear had waded up to its shoulders into the river and was straining to get a better look at me. I saw it lift its vast head to sniff the air, then – catching a whiff of me – turn and bound out of the water at a surprising pace.

Initially, I felt relieved – until I saw that it was trying to outflank me along the shore, its small, eager eyes fixed on me all the time.

I was lucky enough to have been armed – although my gun was on the shore, far out of reach. Knowing it was my only chance of survival, I crept slowly towards the shore, where my rifle hung from an upturned root.

All the while, the bear kept coming, waving his nose around in search of my scent but unable to get a really good sniff as I was downwind. This bought me valuable time.

I loaded my rifle with a shivering hand and readied myself for whatever might come – which turned out to be a full-blown attack.

Finally, this huge killer dropped to all fours and began to bound towards me along the river bank at full tilt.

As long as I live, I will never forget the sight of that powerful animal charging towards me, its nostrils flared and its teeth bared. This bear moved with the speed and agility of a cat – and I had only a couple of rounds with which to stop him.

Suddenly, however, he veered sideways and disappeared into the scrub – and I lowered the rifle, light-headed with relief. But then I heard crashing within the bush. He was now coming at me through the thick undergrowth.

Reluctant to shoot unless it was my only option, I began shouting, making as much noise as possible in an attempt to scare him off.

And up to a point, it worked. He slowed down and then stopped uncertainly, peering at

▶▶

me from just a few yards away. In that moment we were both making a decision.

He was sizing me up before making a final, probably fatal lunge; I was trying to establish whether I could keep my cool for long enough to get off that vital round. Neither of us moved.

For minutes. Three, maybe four – it seemed like hours. And then, with a snort, he turned slowly round and lumbered back into the bush. I felt like the most fortunate man alive.

From the *Daily Mail*, 26 November 2009

Exercise 3

Read the following passage about women's football that you have already seen in Chapter 3 and then write a summary in which you explain how Twitter and other types of social media have helped to popularise the sport. (Note the wording of the question carefully – you are not required to summarise the whole passage.)

Women footballers bring new life to the beautiful game and score with Twitter

Tracy McVeigh

After years of feeling underrated and overlooked by mainstream football pundits and press, women's football is coming into its own this season thanks to social media.

New research shows that the women's version of the game is now the third biggest team sport in the UK in terms of participation, behind only men's football and cricket.

Its previous lack of recognition is being overcome by fans turning to social networking to follow the sport. The second ever season of the Football Association's Women's Super League (WSL) kicks off on Sunday, and eight of England's top female footballers, one from each of the top clubs, will take the unprecedented step of wearing their success on their sleeve by displaying their Twitter account names on their kit.

The new semi-professional league, the top tier of women's football, was launched by the FA last year as a platform to drive forward the women's game and the association claims that it will be spending £3m on promotion in the first three years of the league.

Since the WSL launched, attendances have increased by more than 600%; viewing figures of live broadcast matches, at 450 000, are on a par with those of the men's Scottish Premier League, and the social media channels now attract more than 80 000 followers. It has transformed the player–fan relationship by making it a fully interactive league. Research commissioned for the FA by Sport England Active People ahead of the 2012 season shows that the low profile of women's football is what is driving fans to Twitter and Facebook for news. Fans are up to seven times as interactive as those of the men's game.

The Fifa women's world cup was the most tweeted-about event in the world in July 2011 with 7196 tweets per second at its peak. It remains seventh in the list of the most tweets per second, above the Uefa Champions League in 11th position.

But the findings show that while there are 12 times as many news articles with mentions of women's football per month, relative to the number of people who attend matches; men's football receives three times as many headlines, relative to the number of fans who attend.

'It is understandable in a way,' said England international and Arsenal Ladies midfielder Steph Houghton. 'It's difficult because the men's game is so big and attracts so much money and sponsorship and so it's always going to take priority.'

'But with digital media we can really forge ahead. We don't need to struggle to get a few lines in a newspaper, we can do it for ourselves; fans can interact with players and find out about fixtures and get really involved on match days – even if they are not at the game themselves.'

Houghton, 23, has been selected as the FA WSL digital ambassador for Arsenal Ladies this season. Each club in the league will pick one player who will wear their Twitter address.

'Twitter and Facebook have helped us massively, it's just transformed things over the past year,' Houghton said. 'It's really progressing the game. Our attendance figures have increased a lot. We're doing a lot of work in schools getting girls to play football, breaking down any taboos there might be, and we're seeing them get interested, and bring their families along where they have such a good match day experience that they're coming back.'

'I think that what's happening is that girls are enjoying playing. It's a lot more acceptable and now we have a Women's Super League with hugely dedicated female role models – really committed players who people can see are dedicated and training as hard if not harder than any male players – that's all progressing the sport. And with social media there's no holding women's football back.'

From the *Observer*, 7 April 2012

Exercise 4

Read carefully the passage that follows and write a summary of how advertising developed from the seventeenth century to the present day.

Early advertising

Although word of mouth, the most basic (and still the most powerful) form of advertising, has been around ever since humans started providing each other with goods and services, advertising as a discrete form is generally agreed to have begun alongside newspapers, in the seventeenth century. Frenchman Théophraste Renaudot (Louis XIII's official physician) created a very early version of the supermarket noticeboard, a 'bureau des addresses et des rencontres'. Parisians seeking or offering jobs, or wanting to buy or sell goods, put notices at the office on Île de la Cité. So that the maximum number of people had access to this information, Renaudot created *La Gazette* in 1631, the first French newspaper. The personal ad was born. ▶▶

In England, line advertisements in newspapers were very popular in the second half of the seventeenth century, often announcing the publication of a new book, or the opening of a new play. The Great Fire of London in 1666 was a boost to this type of advertisement, as people used newspapers in the aftermath of the fire to advertise lost and found, and changes of address. These early line ads were predominantly informative, containing descriptive, rather than persuasive language.

Advertisements were of key importance, even at this early point in their history, when it came to informing consumers about new products. Coffee is one such example. Coffee was first brewed into a drink in the Middle East, in the fifteenth century. The Arabs kept the existence of this vivifying concoction a secret, refusing to export beans (or instructions on how to grind and brew them). Legend has it that Sufi Baba Budan smuggled seven beans into India in 1570 and planted them. Coffee then spread to Italy, and throughout Europe, served at coffeehouses. The rapid spread of coffee as both a drink and a pattern of behaviour (coffeehouses became social gathering places) is in no small part due to the advertising of coffee's benefits in newspapers.

When goods were hand-made, by local craftsmen, in small quantities, there was no need for advertising. Buyer and seller were personally known to one another, and the buyer was likely to have direct experience of the product. The buyer also had much more contact with the production process, especially for items like clothing (hand-stitched to fit) and food (assembled from simple, raw ingredients). Packaging and branding were unknown and unnecessary before the Industrial Revolution. However, once technological advances enabled the mass production of soap, china, clothing, etc., the close personal links between buyer and seller were broken. Rather than selling out of their back yards to local customers, manufacturers sought markets a long way from their factories, sometimes on the other side of the world.

This created a need for advertising. Manufacturers needed to explain and recommend their products to customers whom they would never meet personally. Manufacturers, in chasing far-off markets, were beginning to compete with each other. Therefore they needed to brand their products, in order to distinguish them from one another, and create mass recommendations to support the mass production and consumption model.

Newspapers provided the ideal vehicle for this new phenomenon, advertisements. New technologies were also making newspapers cheaper, more widely available, and more frequently printed. They had more pages, so they could carry more, bigger, advertisements. Simple descriptions, plus prices, of products served their purpose until the mid-nineteenth century, when technological advances meant that illustrations could be added to advertising, and colour was also an option. Advertisers started to add copy under the simple headings, describing their products using persuasive prose.

An early advertising success story is that of Pears Soap. Thomas Barratt married into the famous soap-making family and realised that they needed to be more aggressive about pushing their products if they were to survive. He bought the copyright to a painting by noted Pre-Raphaelite artist Sir John Everett Millais, originally entitled 'Bubbles'. Barratt added a bar of Pears Soap to the bottom left of the image, and emblazoned the company name across the top, launching the series of ads featuring cherubic children which firmly welded the brand to the values it still holds today. He took images considered as 'fine art' and used them to connote his brand's quality, purity (i.e. untainted by commercialism) and simplicity (cherubic children). The campaign was a huge success.

Taken from *Mediaknowall*

Exercise 5

Read carefully the passage on page 75 about 'Noise' which you have seen before in Chapter 2. You have been asked to give a talk to your class about the dangers that can be caused by excessive noise. Make notes of the main points you would make and then write the words of your talk as a summary of the passage.

Noise

Noise is a form of pollution which can be merely irritating, or cause physical or emotional damage. For some people, the sound of music played very loudly is annoying, while others revel in it. Similarly, it may be enjoyable for some to drive a motor bike, while other people find the noise anti-social.

Long-term exposure to loud noise can bring about stress which has physical signs such as an increase in oxygen consumption and heart rate, possibly leading to effects on the heart and circulation. Tiredness, irritability and sleep disturbances may also occur.

The physical effects of noise on the ears can be serious. Prolonged, loud noise causes physical discomfort; it actually 'hurts the ears'. And if it is too loud or goes on for too long, it, at first, causes temporary hearing loss, then deafness, due to permanent damage to the delicate mechanism of the inner ear. Rock musicians performing in front of very powerful speakers frequently have permanent hearing damage.

Excessive noise can have a serious effect on health, and is associated with stress and anxiety. Very loud noise causes physical damage to the delicate structures in the ear and may result in deafness.

140 — DANGER TO UNPROTECTED EAR
130 — PAIN THRESHOLD
120
110
100
90
80
70
60
50
40
30
20
10
0

HEARING THRESHOLD

TYPICAL NOISE LEVELS DECIBELS

If used at too high a volume, MP3 players can cause severe hearing loss. Although the speakers are so tiny that they can fit inside the ear, the sound they produce is directed straight down the ear canal and can cause damage if the volume is turned up too high.

Don't underestimate the harmful effects of noise. It is the form of pollution which has the most immediate effect on people. It can cause severe stress.

From *The Environment and Health*, by Brian Ward, Franklin Watts, and *Wake Up to What You Can Do for the Environment*, DETR, 1989

Exercise 6

Read carefully the following passage about how to protect young children from pool accidents. Imagine that you work for the local Health and Safety Department and you have been asked to give a talk to parents about the dangers of swimming pools and what can be done to prevent them.

Make notes of what you want to say and then use them to write the words of your talk, as a summary of the passage.

Protecting children from pool accidents

A child's risk of drowning is much greater than most people realise, especially in residential pools.

Pools are great fun, terrific for cooling down on a hot day and for getting aerobic exercise. But they are also a responsibility. As residential pools have proliferated, so, unfortunately, has the opportunity for tragedy.

While in recent years there has been a decline in drownings among teenage boys in the United States, most of whom succumb in natural bodies of water, there has been no comparable drop in drowning deaths among young children, most of whom succumb in pools – usually the family's pool.

A child's risk of drowning is much greater than most people realise.

Children under the age of five are 14 times as likely to die in a pool as in a motor vehicle. Of those who survive near-drownings, many are permanently brain damaged.

Yet, while the vast majority of parents take care to secure their young children in car seats, far fewer take comparable precautions around pools.

Instead of adopting proven safety measures to prevent pool accidents, too many parents, grandparents and others who have residential pools rely on things like admonitions about not going near the pool alone, the false security of swimming lessons and flotation devices for toddlers, and their sincere but often misguided belief that they will watch closely and constantly when a child is in or near the pool.

A study revealed telling circumstances surrounding the pool-related deaths of young children. Two-thirds occurred in the family pool and one-third in pools owned by friends or relatives.

Nearly half the children were last seen in the house and nearly a quarter were last seen in the yard or on the porch or patio; no one knew the youngsters had gone near the pool.

Only about one-third of the children were in or around the pool just before drowning. Finally, more than three-fourths of the children had been seen five minutes or less before being missed and subsequently found in the pool.

The lessons to be learned from these statistics include the facts that drowning accidents happen very quickly, in familiar surroundings and during very short lapses in supervision.

There are no cries for help to alert caretakers that a small child is in trouble in the water. The only effective protection is to ensure that children cannot get near a pool without being accompanied by a responsible and trained caretaker whose attention is not distracted by phone calls, door bells, reading matter or the care of other children who are not in the pool.

Adopting proven safety measures is a better alternative to the false security of swimming lessons and flotation devices.

While many communities have safety regulations governing residential pools, it is the pool owner's responsibility to follow them. Regardless of local laws, to minimise the risk of pool accidents every owner should adopt these minimal safety standards:

- Fence it in. A fence or comparable barrier completely surrounding the pool is the best preventive, reducing the risk of pool drownings by about 70 per cent, an Australian study showed. It is just as important to fence in an above-ground pool as an in-ground pool, since a small child can easily climb the ladder and fall into the water.
- Cover it.
- Remain vigilant. Children in or near pools must be watched constantly by a responsible and well-informed caretaker. A moment's lapse can spell disaster. Never assume that a child who has taken swimming lessons or is using a flotation device can safely be left unattended, even just to answer the door. For added security when the caretaker is not nearby in the water, children who are not good swimmers could wear properly fitted flotation vests, which keep their heads above water.
- Prepare for emergencies. In addition to the standard ladders or steps to help people climb out of pools, there should be a circular buoy on a rope, a long-handled hook and a rescue ladder at the poolside. A poolside telephone with emergency phone numbers posted next to it is both a convenience and a critical safety feature. Anyone in charge of children playing in or near water should be trained in cardiopulmonary resuscitation and be prepared to use it the moment a child is pulled from the water. Waiting for emergency personnel to arrive can doom a nearly-drowned child.
- Observe other safety measures. Keep toys like tricycles and balls away from pools. Do not permit horseplay in the water. Children should not be allowed to dunk each other, push each other into the water or yell in jest for help. Mark the pool's deep end and, preferably, use a floating pool rope to denote where the water would be above the children's chins. Never permit diving at the shallow end or from the sides of the pool or into an above-ground pool.

From the New Straits Times, 5 July 1994

Becoming a better writer

Your Cambridge IGCSE Second Language English examination at both Core and Extended levels will test your skills in writing English accurately as well as your skills in understanding what someone else has written. Overall, an equal number of marks will be allocated to the reading and writing tasks that you must complete.

At both levels, some of the marks for the summary question will be awarded for how well you have expressed yourself in writing in English. In addition to this, there will be two more questions on each paper for which the quality of your writing will be assessed. At Core level, you will be expected to write 100–150 words for **each** of these tasks. At Extended level you will be expected to write 150–250 words for **each** task.

At both levels, the two writing questions will require you to write in two different registers: formal and informal. One of the questions is likely to be supported by an illustration that may give you some ideas about what to write. This question will also contain bullet points that will help you to structure your response. However, it is important that you do not just repeat the details they give but develop the ideas. A further question will present you with a situation (context) and an audience for your writing. This question will also contain some brief examples of comments that will help you to think about what to write. In both tasks you should try to use a vocabulary and tone that are suited to your audience.

There will be a range of possible types of writing including completing a form, writing a postcard/short letter and a more extended piece of writing. The tasks will require you to describe, report and give personal information. It is unlikely that you will be expected to write argumentatively or to produce an imaginative piece of writing such as a short story. However, in order to help you develop your writing skills, in this chapter we will look at a wider range of genres than just those required specifically for the examination.

Assessment objectives for writing

The writing questions in the examination will test your ability to:

W1 communicate clearly, accurately and appropriately
W2 convey information and express opinions effectively
W3 employ and control a variety of grammatical structures
W4 demonstrate knowledge and understanding of a range of appropriate vocabulary
W5 observe conventions of paragraphing, punctuation and spelling
W6 employ appropriate register/style.

Whenever you write anything (either for an English examination or for any other purpose) it is important to keep in mind that what you write may be read by someone who has never met you and has no knowledge of your personality or circumstances. It is, therefore, very important that you try to express yourself as clearly as you can so that the reader can understand the ideas or information that you are communicating. Whatever piece of writing you try, you need to **think about its purpose** and decide what effect this has on your writing style. There are two key questions to ask yourself before you start writing.

- **What is it for?** In other words, what kind of writing piece is it (it could be anything from a fantasy story to a business letter) and what do you want to say? You should try to **use different styles for different purposes**.
- **Who is it for?** Who are the readers for this piece of writing? You need to be able to **use different styles for different audiences**.

Even when we think about just one kind of writing task – a letter, for example – the style will need to be different depending on who the letter is for (a relative? a newspaper? a friend?). When you write an article you need to think about your readers: if it is for a group of young people, for instance, you need to think about how to make it clear and interesting for them, not just about what information you want to include.

Remember: some examination questions will tell you who the audience is for your answer, but you shouldn't forget that as well as the given audience there is another person, the examiner, who will be reading what you have written!

Different styles for different purposes

Writing to inform or explain

One of the writing questions in your Cambridge IGCSE Second Language English examination will require you to produce a piece of factual writing, for example to inform or explain. With this kind of writing it is important to be as clear as possible, whether you are explaining a situation, an activity or an interest, or providing some instructions for carrying out a task. Make sure your writing is **focused** and **objective**, **clear** and **systematic**.

Be focused and objective

Your purpose is to make the information clear to your readers, not to give them your own opinion on the subject, so stick closely to the subject and don't be tempted to add comments of your own.

Be clear and systematic

The point of an explanation is that it should be simpler and clearer than the original. Here are some techniques to help you achieve this.

- Use vocabulary that is easy to understand.
- If you are answering a directed writing question which is based on a passage that is printed on the question paper, be careful not simply to repeat chunks of the original text; instead, find simpler ways to express the same ideas so that you are genuinely explaining them.
- Use sentences that are not too long or complicated.
- Make sure your punctuation is accurate and helpful so that readers can easily see their way from one point to the next.
- Use a new paragraph for every main point that you make: start the paragraph with a 'topic sentence' to tell your reader what the paragraph will be about and use the rest of the paragraph to develop the point.

Examples of informative writing

The next two passages are examples of writing that informs and explains.

The passage below is aimed at passengers travelling from Schiphol Airport in Amsterdam in the Netherlands. It gives information as to how to check in for the Dutch KLM Airline.

Read through it carefully and then look at the teacher's comments, which explain the key features of this type of writing.

The heading is clear and explains concisely the purpose of the leaflet.

Checking in at the airport

Unable to check in online? Then check in at one of the self-service check-in machines at the airport and hand your baggage over at one of the baggage drop-off points.

Checking in

The vocabulary used is direct and straightforward (not all travellers may speak English very well) but the use of 'you' and 'your' helps to create an informal and friendly tone.

Headings are used to help take the readers logically through the check-in process step by step.

Again the simplicity of the process is emphasised and all necessary information is given in a concise and easily understandable manner.

Checking in online is the fastest and simplest way of checking in. If you are unable to check in online, you can still check in at one of our self-service check-in machines at the airport. These can be found at the entrance to counters 14/15 at Amsterdam Airport Schiphol.

In just a couple of easy steps you can check in yourself and your travelling companions. As when you check in online, you can choose your favourite seat on board.

This is how the self-service check-in machine works:

Step 1

Insert your passport or frequent flyer card, or enter your ticket number or booking code. Your booking details will appear on the screen.

Step 2

Select your seat on the seating map. You can also buy a seat in the Economy Comfort zone, a seat with extra legroom, or a preferred seat. Alternatively, you can treat yourself to an upgrade to World Business Class! All it takes is a credit card to make the change.

Step 3

Print your boarding pass.

Step 4

Do you have check-in baggage? Simply hand it over at the nearest baggage drop-off point, and proceed to the gate. Have a good trip!

If you are already checked in, you can also use the self-service check-in machines to print your boarding pass. They are available round the clock at Amsterdam Airport Schiphol. At most other airports, the self-service check-in machines are available for checking in and printing boarding passes at least two hours before flight departure.

Check-in for flights to Asia

You can also use our self-service machines in Chinese, Korean and Japanese. These languages are also spoken by our assistants at the gate. They are gladly available for translation of all announcements made, and to help you with any questions before boarding.

A diagram is used to reinforce the written information and to help to ensure that passengers know where they should go.

Check-in desks

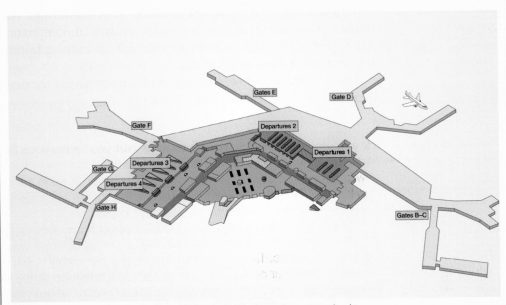

Overview of Amsterdam Airport Schiphol's departure terminals

The information is completed with details of how to check in for passengers not wanting to use the automatic machines.

You can also check in at the check-in desks for flights departing the same day. The check-in desks at Amsterdam Airport Schiphol are open from 5:00a.m. from Tuesday to Thursday and from 4:30a.m. from Friday to Monday. Our check-in desk staff are also happy to help you should you only have a question.

Baggage drop-off point

If you have already checked in, you only need to hand over your check-in baggage at one of the baggage drop-off points at the airport. These can be found at the entrance to counters 12/13 at Amsterdam Airport Schiphol. Most airports accept your baggage up to 2 hours before your flight departs on the day of departure.

You will be issued a baggage claim tag for every bag that you check in. Make sure to save these tags until you have received your baggage at your destination.

From *www.klm.com*

Exercise 1

Re-read the information on pages 80–81 about how to check in at Schiphol Airport and then attempt the following task.

Your grandparents are planning to fly from Schiphol to visit friends living in Japan. They are not very experienced in travelling by plane and have asked you, as someone who flies frequently, for advice on how they should check in. They have a computer at home.

Write a letter to your grandparents in which you inform them about the check-in procedure.

Your letter should be about 150 words long. You should use the information in the leaflet but use your own words and do not copy from it. Remember to write in a tone appropriate to a letter to close relatives. You do not need to give your address.

Exercise 2

The tasks which follow this passage will help you to prepare for the informative writing tasks that you will come across in your Cambridge IGCSE Second Language English examination, although they are not actual examination questions. You will also find that you will need to use your skills in making notes and summarising to be able to answer them successfully.

Read the article below, which provides information for new users of Twitter and then answer the questions that follow.

If you want to take the Twitter plunge, but you're nervous to make the first step, follow our simple guide to getting started

Twitter is a social networking service that allows you to send out short text messages up to 140 characters to your friends and followers. It's a great way to spread news and engage and communicate with a group of people.

Twitter gives you the opportunity to connect with people and places you admire.

There are 10 million Twitter users in the UK, many of which tweet on the move via their smartphones. Twitter provides a running commentary to live events and goes into overdrive for major occasions such as concerts, television series finales and sporting fixtures. Major news stories explode on Twitter and in the last year we have seen key world events unrolling in live tweets.

Get started

The first hurdle is to decide on your name or Twitter handle, write a short biography and upload a photograph. If you have a blog, it's worth keeping your names consistent. If you're tweeting for business then create a specific handle. Once you've signed up, get your Twitter legs by sending out your first tweet – you can always go back and change your picture and biography. Start by writing a tweet or click reply to a tweet from a friend to start chatting. Photographs and links are a great way to get the conversation rolling. You can follow discussions without having to tweet and there are lots of people who use it in this way.

Who to follow?

Who you follow is completely down to personal taste. Twitter gives you the opportunity to connect with people and places you admire. Start by following your friends and family members, then add your interests such as the handles for television programmes, events, and your favourite brands. In addition, Twitter will recommend people for you to follow.

Generally, the more you tweet the more followers you gain. Popular celebrities have large followings running into milions. It might take a while for you to reach this level of followers though!

Safety tips

Remember that Twitter is in the public domain so as a rule of thumb don't say anything on Twitter that you wouldn't say in public. Be careful sharing personal information and if you receive any unwanted tweets you can quickly block the follower. There's lots more information on safety in Twitter's help centre.

Twitter is a light-hearted, friendly place and a fun way to connect with people and places you enjoy and admire. Tweet about what you love and you'll attract like-minded followers.

If you found this feature helpful, please tweet it to your friends.

Glossary of Twitter terms

From the school gate to the news room, the words *tweets*, *trends* and *hashtags* are regularly dropped into everyday conversation. Get to grips with the terminology with our jargon-busting guide.

Tweet: A 140-character message.
Feed: The stream of tweets you see on your homepage. It's the easy way to read updates from the people you follow.
Retweet (RT): You can 'retweet' a message if you like it, find it funny or newsworthy and want to share it with your followers. The tweet is marked with RT.
@mention: The @mention is a way to communicate with another user in a tweet (e.g. @hodderbooks). @mention is public and anyone can access conversations by clicking on the @name.
Direct Message (DM): A private, 140-character message between two people. You may only DM a user who follows you.
Hashtag (#): The # symbol, called a hashtag, is used to mark keywords or conversation in a tweet. The hashtag is a discovery tool that allows you to participate in a wider conversation or others to find your tweets. Click on the hashtag and you will see all the latest tweets on that topic – including tweets from people you don't follow.
Trends: A snapshot of the most popular conversations happening on Twitter at that moment. You can choose to view trends in your local area, UK or worldwide.

From *www.tescomagazine.com*

Task 1

Your favourite auntie, who is 62 years old, has decided that she wants to become a user of Twitter. She has a reasonable understanding of modern technology and owns a PC and a cell phone. She has asked you for advice on how to set up and use a Twitter account. Write a letter to her in which you explain what Twitter is and how she should get started with using it. The tone of your letter should be both informative and friendly. Plan your letter by making a list of the main points that you will use before you start to write.

You should use your own words as far as possible and not just copy whole phrases from the article.

Task 2

As an experienced user of Twitter, you have been asked by a youth group to which you belong to talk to parents of younger members (13/14 years old) of the group to explain to them and give them information about what Twitter is, in order to help them decide whether they should allow their children to be involved in using the service. Plan your talk by making a list of the main points that you will use before you start to write.

You should use your own words as far as possible and not just copy whole phrases from the article.

Remember that for both of the tasks you must use only the information contained in the article above. You should not use any other knowledge that you may have, even if you are an experienced user of Twitter!

Writing to persuade

When you are writing factually, it is important that the main purpose of what you write is to convey facts and details as clearly and straightforwardly as you can. However, not all the writing you will do in preparation for your Cambridge IGCSE examination will require you to write in this way. It is very likely that one of the questions will require you to present an argument or to persuade your readers to share a particular point of view.

When writing to persuade, you should try to use language in a slightly different way. It is likely that it will be more complex and emotively-toned, with vocabulary chosen to influence your readers' feelings and not just to convey facts to them. Although it is important that you should use facts and statistics to back up your argument, it is likely that you will adapt the facts in order to try to make your argument as convincing as you can, rather than simply allowing the readers to make up their own minds about them.

Writing to argue or persuade needs to be **convincing and logical**. Here are some useful techniques.

- Decide **what** you want to persuade your reader to believe. Which viewpoint are you going to put forward?
- Make 'for and against' lists: one list of the facts and ideas which support your viewpoint, and another list of those which do not.

> **Note:** You can change your chosen viewpoint at this planning stage, but don't change it as you are writing!

- State your chosen viewpoint simply at the beginning.
- For each main point that you make to support your viewpoint, **give evidence and examples** to back up your case – **use the text if your answer is in response to one**.
- **Be balanced** – your argument will be at its most convincing if you make points for both sides but prove that your own chosen viewpoint is the better one. Use your 'for and against' lists.
- Use paragraphs to help you make your points clearly. Start a new paragraph for each main point that you make and use the rest of the paragraph to give your evidence. This will mean that your paragraphs are of roughly similar lengths.
- Use persuasive phrases such as: 'It seems clear to me that …', 'The text shows that …', 'This example indicates that …'.
- Use linking phrases to move between the two sides of the argument, such as: 'Nevertheless, …'; 'On the other hand, …'.
- Rhetorical questions are a good way to get your reader on your side: these are questions which have an obvious answer, and the answer supports your point of view! For example, if you were arguing against animal experiments, you could ask: 'Would you like your own pets to have shampoo squirted into their eyes?' If you were arguing in favour of animal experiments, you could ask: 'Your little brother is dangerously ill – would you rather he had drugs whose safety had been tested on animals, or no drugs?'
- Finish by restating your viewpoint, perhaps saying also that, although you can see the other point of view, you are convinced that yours is the right one.

Example of argumentative/persuasive writing

The article that follows is an example of a piece of argumentative writing and was produced by a 14-year-old school student. In it the writer is attempting to argue in favour of wearing school uniform.

Read through the article carefully and then look at the teacher's comments.

Well, I think we should wear school uniforms.

Firstly, because it gives a sense of uniformity. When wearing the same clothing, we all look as if everyone is equally the same and those who are poor would feel like they have 'fitted-in' to their studying environment. Some others, even the rich people, may want to find some way to fit into society, so perhaps this would be one way of doing so.

Secondly, you don't have to choose your outfit every day. Although I do understand, some may say 'What about Saturdays and Sundays when you don't have to go to school?' My response would be 'well, at least you don't have to choose for the majority of the days in the week'. So it minimises those 'time-consuming' decisions on choosing an outfit (by choosing an outfit, I mean that some people can be a little picky on choosing their outfit, especially those who want to look better and rise above their ranks).

Thirdly, it gives identification. For example, if you are from XYZ, people in the streets or anywhere else can easily identify that you are (insert your name here). So, if you are lost when you are on a school excursion, teachers, passers-by can easily identify you.

Now, I understand that some uniforms can be a little uncomfortable, especially for the unfortunate ones. That can't be solved, unless certain schools allow you to adjust your uniforms.

Next, you can't show off your personality. I do agree with this, and it is somewhat important in certain societies. However, I do believe schools are as much concerned with education as well as with making lifelong leaders and wearing clothing that expresses one's personality may cause jealousy, which may affect a student's education and chance to lead in the future.

Furthermore, some may say 'those who are poor can't afford their uniforms'. Certain countries have special funds provided by the ministry to allow them to purchase the uniforms. For those countries which don't, I'm sure the school would understand and maybe give them a set of their

The writer's viewpoint is clearly stated here.

A practical example is given to support the statement.

In this section the writer gives consideration to the arguments of people opposed to wearing uniform but also states reasons for thinking otherwise.

This phrase effectively links this paragraph with what has gone before.

▶▶

uniform to wear. I don't believe that a school will not treat each of their students equally. (If they do then I am sorry for you.)

Speaking from where I am, my school and other neighbouring schools do not treat everyone unequally. Everyone is given the opportunity to study well or to lead, it's up to the students whether they want it or not.

Some of you would say 'Hey, those schools of a higher rank (those requiring good grades to enter) would bully the ones who wear uniforms of a lower rank school!' The truth is, even if you wear or do not wear your uniforms, you still get bullied either way. The percentage may be different, but it's very close to being equal. For example, if you wear a uniform, and you do something stupid which gives the opportunity for bullies to bully you it's the same as if you wear something that is old and tattered, or even not up with the current fashion, you'll still get bullied, won't you?

One of the major reasons for people to oppose this is out of a sense of freedom or fairness. Yes, I do understand this. However, sometimes there are things in life that you are restricted to, such as laws and rules and regulations which keep you in shape. As a student, I agree, I do feel that I don't have my freedom – the tie I have to wear makes me feel like I'm a dog on a leash – but I have started to realise that certain restrictions do help us. For example, wearing ties seemed to be a bore, a tradition I used to hate, but now I realise that it was to help us as it shows a sense of formality, discipline and respect to oneself and others.

Lastly, some people say, 'It's just a piece of clothing. How does it help at all? It's generally USELESS'. I do agree it's just a piece of clothing, but I do believe there is a meaning for it, a significance, even if it may be a hidden meaning. It shows that we are united, we are together as a school. Our dignity, our potential is actually all the same despite our differences in status. Unity is better than separation, two heads are better than one. Don't you agree?

Just some last words. I'm only a 14-year-old student. I may not understand all the arguments but these are my thoughts in favour of school uniform at this moment in time and I realise that there are many specific and powerful reasons to wear or not to wear uniform. But remember, this is just a debate. I don't mean to offend, or say that 'There can only be one right answer. Which is Yes'. I just want to share my views and that's that. I would like to hear your views as well. That's all for now from me. :D

From *www.forandagainst.com*

Notice how each paragraph contains a new main point which is then developed.

A rhetorical question is used to support the writer's viewpoint.

This paragraph restates the writer's viewpoint and also acknowledges that others may think differently and this is an ongoing topic of discussion. It is an effective conclusion to the article.

Exercise 1

1 Re-read the article on pages 85–86 and then make a list of the points *against* wearing school uniform that the writer makes. Add any further points of your own that you can think of to the list.
2 Now use these notes to write a letter to the writer of the original article to convince her/him that wearing school uniform is not a good thing. (This should be a friendly letter and you should make up a name for the person to whom you are writing.)

Exercise 2

The tasks that make up this exercise require you to practise a range of skills that will help you to prepare for the questions in the Cambridge IGCSE English Second Language examination. Your teacher will advise on how best to approach the tasks and whether you should attempt all or just some of them. You may wish to complete the work as a group exercise with each member of the group working on a different task.

Printed on pages 87–90 are four articles (A–D) concerning endangered animals. Passage A is a blog written by a secondary school student and states some general points about why we should be concerned with protecting threatened species. Passages B–D are concerned specifically with one seriously endangered species, the Asiatic lion, and contain a range of information about the animal.

Read all four articles carefully before completing the tasks that follow.

Passage A

You're in a city, walking around town like any other day, and you don't come across a single person. Have they all died? Where have they gone? Friends, family, just disappearing? Is the quote 'If I was the last person in the world' funny anymore? This is called extinction. Thousands of species are threatened – animals you would never know are endangered, along with thousands more. Animals like the polar bear, tigers, birds of all kinds, pandas, monkeys, elephants, and even butterflies are dealing with losing their own kind. These things are important and shouldn't be taken lightly.

Many endangered animals are dying because they can't survive without having their habitats like forests that provide food and shelter. Why does this happen, is there a reason? These things are happening because industries and businesses cut down the forest for making resources and to gather wood for building, but they are taking away animals' natural habitats. In addition, littering, oil spills in the ocean, global warming, taking animals out of their habitats for zoos or to make them pets all cause extinction. This is killing the animals and is not acceptable. Animals have a right to be here just as much as we do.

When an animal dies, it ruins our ecosystem. How? Let's say bees became extinct; nothing would collect the pollen. It would get over produced, making it bad for the air and making people sick. Along with tigers – if tigers were gone, they wouldn't be hunting antelope and other animals any longer, which would result in these animals over populating. The world needs animals for reasons like this.

People disagree with animals becoming extinct because they think there is a natural reason for this, but fortunately that's not the case at all. They're dying because we are killing them. That just shows you, if we don't take action now, they might not be here one day. They have a right to be here. More should be done to protect them. If it seems so easy to take their lives then it should be easy to save them.

From jade4402.edublogs.org

Passage B

Endangered Species: The Asiatic Lion

Scientific name: *Panthera leo persica*
Group: Mammals
Status/date listed as endangered: EN-US FWS: 2 June 1970
Area(s) where listed as endangered: Turkey to India

The Asiatic lion is a subspecies of the lion found in Senegal east to Somalia, East Africa, Angola, northern Namibia and from Kalahari east to Mozambique and northern Natal. Asiatic lions are generally smaller than African lions, and the most noticeable difference is the long fold of skin running along the Asiatic lion's belly that is rarely found on the African lion. Adults can reach up to 1.8 metres in head and body length, their tails reaching up to 1 metre in length. Females are smaller than males. The males can weigh up to 250 kilos and the females can weigh up to 180 kilos. Their fur is tan in colour and is a great camouflage in the light-coloured savanna grasses. The mane of the males varies in colour from light to dark brown or even black, and it is generally shorter than that of the African lion making their ears more visible.

The Asiatic lion prefers grassy plains, savanna, and open woodlands as its habitat. Like African lions, they are very social and live in groups called 'prides'. Asiatic lion prides are smaller than African lion prides, and males prefer to associate with the pride when mating or during hunting. They are nocturnal creatures, and most of the day is spent resting. Asiatic lions prey on medium to large mammals, such as deer and gazelles, and young elephants, rhinos, and hippos. Breeding can occur year-round and females give birth to one to five cubs after a gestation period of 100 to 119 days.

Asiatic lion populations have suffered due to sport hunting in the 1800s (until it was outlawed) and habitat loss due to the clearing of jungle forest for extracting wood and human settlement. The Gir, a national park and lion sanctuary, has been successful in stabilising one of the last remaining wild populations. Also, the species does well in captivity and some are found in zoos.

From Glenn, C.R. 2006. 'Earth's Endangered Creatures – Asiatic Lion Facts' (Online). Accessed 9/17/2013 at *http://earthsendangered.com*

Passage C

Critically endangered lion now found only in India

The Asiatic lion (*Panthera leo persica*) is a subspecies of the lion now found only in India.

Asiatic lions once ranged from the Mediterranean to India, covering most of West Asia where it was also known as the Persian lion.

Their numbers range between 250–300.

Their main prey species consist of nilgai, chital, sambhar, goats, buffaloes and occasionally also other smaller animals.

Compared to its African counterpart, the males of the Indian lion have a scantier mane and a characteristic skin fold at the belly. In fact you can always tell the difference between an African male lion and Asiatic male lion because their ears are always visible, whereas on an African lion they are always hidden by the mane.

Asiatic lions are also slightly smaller than their African cousins, although the largest Asiatic lion on record was an imposing 2.9 m in length.

Though they have a less well developed mane, Asiatic lions have thicker elbow tufts and a longer tail tuft.

Lions, unlike the tiger, are communal and hunt in groups. They collectively stalk their prey and have been commonly seen applying strategies that would do any army commander proud.

The prey is mostly killed by a quick, powerful bite to the spine or with the help of a classic choke grip, with the strong jaws of the lion cutting off air supply to the lungs.

Seemingly there is only one known wild population that can be found in Gir Forest National Park in India.

It is critically endangered and there are fears about inbreeding. However, the chances of seeing one in the wild (in the Gir Forest National Park) are seemingly good.

From *wwf.panda.org*

Passage D

Asian Lion

Only 200 or so Asian lions exist in the wild. A former royal reserve, India's Gir Forest, is the last home of this lion subspecies.

Nearly all wild lions live in sub-Saharan Africa, but one small population of Asian lions exists in India's Gir Forest. Asian lions and African lions are subspecies of the same species.

Asian lions once prowled from the Middle East to India. Now, only 200 to 260 of these magnificent animals survive in the wild. The Gir Forest's dry teak woods were once a royal hunting ground. Today they are a reserve where the endangered Asian lions are heavily protected. An additional 200 Asian lions live in zoos.

Size relative to a 6 ft (2 m) man

Lions are the only cats that live in groups, called prides. Prides are family units that may include up to three males, a dozen or so females, and their young. All of a pride's lionesses are related and female cubs typically stay with the group as they age. Young males eventually leave and may establish their own prides by taking over a group headed by another male.

Only male lions boast manes, the impressive fringe of long hair that encircles their heads. Males defend the pride's territory. They mark the area with urine, roar menacingly to warn intruders, and chase off animals that encroach on their turf.

Female lions are the pride's primary hunters. They often work together to prey upon large mammals.

After the hunt, the group effort often degenerates to squabbling over the sharing of the kill, with cubs at the bottom of the pecking order. Young lions do not help the pride hunt until they are about a year old. Lions will hunt alone if the opportunity presents itself, and they also steal kills from hyenas or wild dogs.

From *www.nationalgeographic.com*

Complete the following tasks using information from the articles contained in passages A–D on pages 87–90.

> **Note:** The tasks will test not only your writing skills but also your summary writing and general comprehension.

1 Write a letter to the Editor of a magazine aimed at teenagers. In your letter you should give details about the Asiatic lion, why you consider it is important that it should not be allowed to become extinct and suggest how people of your age can help in saving it.
2 By using details from all of the articles on pages 87–90, write the words of a web-page aimed at pre-teenage children in which you give information about the Asiatic lion and explain what is meant by 'an endangered species'.
3 You listen to a radio phone-in in which one of the callers says that 'if some species of animals die out, it's their problem and is simply the way things are. There's nothing we can do about it.' You strongly disagree with this and call the number to make your feelings known.
   Write the words of what you will say when your call is answered and explain carefully your reasons for disagreeing with the previous speaker. (It is important to make notes of the key points of what you intend to say before writing your answer.)
4 You and your friends are members of a group that are involved in animal welfare. Produce a leaflet for distribution to all people in your local area. The leaflet is intended to raise awareness of the plight of seriously endangered species and to encourage its readers to support your organisation in a variety of ways. (Remember that not everyone who reads the leaflet may hold the same views as you and your friends, so it is important to use facts and details to support your arguments.)

Writing a letter

You may be asked to read some information and write a letter in response. The following are just three examples of the type of letter you might be asked to write:

- a letter giving information or advice to a friend or relative
- a letter to a magazine or newspaper, commenting on the material and giving your reaction
- a letter explaining or apologising for a problem.

As with any piece of writing, remember to think about the **audience** and the **purpose**.

- **Who are you writing to?** This will help you to decide how formal your letter needs to be. If it is a letter to a friend, for instance, it can be in a chatty style and you can use some informal, colloquial language. For example, instead of 'I feel I must express my views on …' it would be more appropriate to say 'I must tell you what I thought about …'.
- **What are you writing for?** Is it to inform, to make a request, to complain, or to explain a particular point of view? The answer to this question will have an effect on how you write. For example, if it is a letter to a company then your points must be clearly ordered and written in a systematic, logical way. One important point: even if your letter is making a complaint about a situation or disagreeing with someone else's opinion, it should never be abusive or rude.
- It is likely that the question will provide you with an outline of the content of your letter but it is important that you adapt this in such a way that it is interesting to the reader and focused clearly on the specific requirements of the task.

How should your letter be set out?

Although the layout of a letter may not be as important as the content, you should follow certain guidelines. Study the layouts for a personal letter and a formal letter on pages 92–93, and use them appropriately. You must set your letter out neatly; there is never any excuse for an untidy-looking letter.

A personal letter to a friend or relative

Put your address at the top right-hand corner, with the date underneath it.

7 Hillside Close
Anytown
Blankshire
AB1 2YZ

1 November 2013

Dear Claire

_____

_____

_____

_____

_____

_____

_____

_____

_____

_____

_____

_____

_____

_____

Use an informal ending.

With love from

A formal letter

Put your address at the top right-hand corner.

7 Hillside Close
Anytown
Blankshire
AB1 2YZ

Put the name and address of the person you are writing to on the left-hand side of the page.

Mr Brown
Head of Leisure Services
Blankshire Council
Council Offices
Anytown
Blankshire
AB4 6JQ

Put the date below this address.

2 November 2013

If you don't know the name of the person you are writing to, start 'Dear Sir/Madam'.

Dear Mr Brown

_____

_____

_____

_____

_____

_____

_____

_____

_____

If you used the person's name at the start of the letter, end with 'Yours sincerely'. If you started the letter 'Dear Sir/Madam', end with 'Yours faithfully'. If you know the person you are writing to quite well, you could end your letter more informally: 'With best wishes', for example.

Yours sincerely

Examples of letters

Read these two letters about an incident in a mini-market. The first is an example of how not to write a letter of apology; the second is much more appropriate in content and tone.

Dear Mrs Arensky,

My parents have made me write this letter though I don't think it's fair. You should blame the person who left the fixture sticking out into the aisle of the shop. You can't blame Minnie for escaping when I dropped her as she doesn't know any better and you can't blame me for chasing after her. And you have to admit it is a bit silly to put all those eggs there. They're just asking to be knocked over, aren't they. You see, Minnie isn't used to having a large space to run around in and I couldn't stop her from running off and did my best to stop her by shouting out to her. Anyway, half the trouble was your shoppers. They didn't look where they were going. So they bumped into each other. I thought it was funny when Mr Lee, a teacher at my school, got trapped against the tins of vegetables and they all collapsed on him. I mean you have to laugh, don't you.

Yours,

Olga Mishkin

No paragraphing and the content is not ordered.

The tone of the letter is all wrong – it is not apologetic but it is complaining.

The content of the letter is distorted as Olga tries to shift the blame.

Given that this is a formal letter, the ending is incorrect. It should be 'Yours sincerely'.

Dear Mrs Arensky,

I would like to apologise for the unfortunate incident that I caused in your mini-market last Thursday. I have talked it over with my parents who have suggested that I write to you to explain how it happened.

I admit that it was my fault in bringing my pet mouse, Minnie, into your shop in the first place. She was in a box as I was taking her to my friend's house as she was going to look after Minnie for me while I was away on a school trip. Unfortunately, as I approached the meat counter, I bumped against one of your fixtures, dropped the box and Minnie escaped. She set off with me behind her. As she scampered around, many of the other shoppers started to panic. One lady screamed and jumped out of the way and, without looking where she was heading, fell into a pile of eggs which crashed to the floor and broke. People started to slip over, and in no time at all there was total disorder. I eventually managed to recapture Minnie who had stopped to eat some soft fruit that another customer had dropped.

Although it was really just an accident, I realised that it is my responsibility to apologise and to offer to pay for the damage. My parents have generously said they will lend me the money which I can pay back over what will probably have to be a very long period of time.

Yours sincerely,

Olga Mishkin

The letter starts by getting straight to the point.

A development paragraph clearly explains exactly what happened.

The third paragraph neatly rounds off the letter with a return to the opening.

The letter started with a name, so the ending is correct.

Writing imaginatively to entertain your readers

The writing tasks that are set for the Cambridge IGCSE Second Language English examination are likely to ask you to write informatively or persuasively. You will not be asked to write a short story or any piece of imaginative fiction under examination conditions.

However, it is very likely that as part of your English course at school your teacher will ask you to write imaginatively at some point. In this section we will look at some of the techniques required for writing imaginatively, some examples of writing of this type and some tasks that you can use to improve your skills. All of this will help to develop your ability to write English fluently and, as a result, will help when you are answering the writing tasks in the examination.

We will look at two specific types of imaginative writing: the first consists of two examples of imaginative descriptive writing and the second is a piece of fiction, a complete short story. Before we look at these passages, however, here are some general points to consider as to what helps to make a good piece of imaginative writing.

Tips for writing imaginatively

If you are writing an imaginative piece – narrating a story, for example – you will not have to structure your piece in the same logical, argued way as for an informative or persuasive piece. However, it is still important that your writing has a clear structure. Perhaps most importantly, you need to know how your story will end before you start (see the section on planning on pages 101–103). You might want your ending to be a surprise to your readers, but it shouldn't be a surprise to you! The beginning is important, too. For a story you can either:

- start by setting the scene – this is fine, but don't give too much time/space to it, keep it to one short paragraph
- go straight into the story, for example with a line of dialogue.

A good piece of imaginative writing is **varied** and **inventive**. Here are some ideas on how to make sure your skills in this area are clear to the reader!

- Use some words which are abstract and colourful.
- Use descriptive vocabulary: adjectives, adverbs.
- Use imagery, for example, 'she grinned like a crocodile'.
- Use exclamations and/or words that convey their meaning through sound. (These might be dramatic, for example, 'Thud!', 'Crash!'; or they might just be well-chosen words that convey the exact sound you have in mind, for example, 'tinkling', 'rustled'.)
- Your paragraphs should vary in length. An occasional very short paragraph can make a strong impact. Some paragraphs might even be just one word long, such as 'Help!'
- Your sentences should also vary in length – this is a good way to have an effect on your reader's feelings. For example, if you have just been setting a frightening scene, a short sentence such as 'We waited.' or even just 'Silence.' can be very effective.

Imaginative descriptions

Passage A is taken from the novel *The Third Policeman* by the Irish writer Flann O'Brien. In this extract the narrator describes breaking into an old, apparently empty house in order to find a black box which he hopes contains something valuable. Read the extract carefully and then carefully read the comments.

Passage A

I opened the iron gate and walked as softly as I could up the weed-tufted gravel drive. My mind was strangely empty. I felt no glow of pleasure and was unexcited at the prospect of becoming rich. I was occupied only with the mechanical task of finding a black box.

The front-door was closed and set far back in a very deep porch. The wind and rain had whipped a coating of gritty dust against the panels and deep into the crack where the door opened, showing that it had been shut for years. Standing on a derelict flower-bed, I tried to push open the first window on the left. It yielded to my strength, raspingly and stubbornly. I clambered through the opening and found myself, not at once in a room, but crawling along the deepest window-ledge I had ever seen. After I had jumped noisily down upon the floor, I looked up and the open window seemed very far away and much too small to have admitted me.

The room where I found myself was thick with dust, musty and empty of all furniture. Spiders had erected great stretchings of their web about the fireplace. I made my way quickly to the hall, threw open the door of the room where the box was and paused on the threshold. It was a dark morning and the weather had stained the windows with blears of grey wash which kept the brightest part of the weak light from coming in. The far corner of the room was a blur of shadow. I had a sudden urge to have done with my task and be out of this house forever. I walked across the bare boards, knelt down in the corner and passed my hands about the floor in search of the loose board. To my surprise I found it easily. It was about two feet in length and rocked hollowly under my hand. I lifted it up, laid it aside and struck a match. I saw a black metal cash-box nestling dimly in the hole. I put my hand down and crooked a finger into the loose reclining handle but the match suddenly flickered and went out and the handle of the box, which I had lifted up about an inch, slid heavily off my finger. Without stopping to light another match, I thrust my hand into the opening and, just when it should be closing about the box, something happened.

From *The Third Policeman* by Flann O'Brien

The choice of the active verb 'whipped' and the adjective 'gritty' produce a clear picture in the reader's mind of the physical appearance of the window and how strongly the dust is stuck to it.

The two adverbs emphasise the difficulty the narrator has in opening the window. 'Raspingly' suggests the sound as the window creaks open and 'stubbornly' implies that it is physically trying to prevent this happening.

This phrase describes the thick spiders' webs that cover the fireplace. Notice how the writer suggests their strength and gives the description greater force by making the spiders actively the subject of the verb 'erected' and using the verbal noun 'stretchings' rather than simply saying 'spiders' webs stretched across the fireplace'.

Again, rather than simply saying 'the corner of the room was in shadow' the writer uses a metaphor 'was a blur of shadow' which makes the description more direct and also suggests that the shadow is a physical, threatening presence.

As the moment of discovery of the box becomes closer, the writer uses a short sentence of 11 words containing three active verbs to build up excitement.

The last two words of this paragraph leave the reader in suspense and waiting to read on to find out what happens next.

In this passage, the writer is describing surroundings that are mysterious and a little creepy. The comments on the highlighted words and phrases give some suggestions as to how he uses language to achieve these effects.

The second passage is taken from *A High Wind in Jamaica* by Richard Hughes and describes a morning in the Caribbean when a group of children are riding to a place called Exeter Rocks on ponies, to spend the day escaping from the heat. The weather is exceptionally calm and extremely hot – it is, in fact, building up to a hurricane.

Read the passage carefully and then answer the questions that follow, which refer to the highlighted sections. Try to make your answers as detailed as you can as gaining a clear understanding of how the writer achieves his effects will help to develop your own descriptive writing skills.

⭐ Passage B

The sun was still red and large: the sky above cloudless, and like blue glaze poured over baking clay: (1) but close over the ground a dirty grey haze hovered. As they followed the lane towards the sea they came to a place where, yesterday, a fair-sized spring had bubbled up by the roadside. Now it was dry. But even as they passed some water splashed out, and then it was dry again, although gurgling inwardly to itself. (2) But the group of children were hot, far too hot to speak to one another: they sat on their ponies as loosely as possible, longing for the sea.

The morning advanced. (3) The heated air grew quite easily hotter, as if from some enormous furnace from which it could draw at will. Bullocks only shifted their stinging feet when they could bear the soil no longer: even the insects were too lethargic to pipe, the basking lizards hid themselves and panted. (4) It was so still you could have heard the least buzz a mile off. Not a naked fish would willingly move his tail. The ponies advanced because they must. The children ceased even to think.

They all very nearly jumped out of their skins; for close at hand a crane [a bird like a stork] had trumpeted once desperately. Then the broken silence closed down as flawless as before. They perspired twice as violently as a result of the sudden noise. (5) Their pace grew slower and slower. It was no faster than a procession of snails when at last they reached the sea.

Exeter Rocks is a famous place. A bay of the sea, almost a perfect semi-circle, guarded by the reef: shelving white sands to span the few feet from the water to the under-cut turf: and then, almost at the mid point, a jutting-out shelf of rocks right into deep water – fathoms deep. And a narrow crack in the rocks, leading the water into a small pool, or miniature lagoon, right inside their stronghold. There it was, safe from sharks or drowning, that the children meant to soak themselves all day, like turtles in a pen. The water of the bay was smooth and unmoving, yet perfectly pure and clear: nevertheless, the swell muttered a mile away on the reef. The water within the pool itself could not reasonably be smoother. No sea-breeze thought of stirring. No bird trespassed on the heavy air. (6)

From A High Wind in Jamaica by Richard Hughes

1 Identify the simile used by the writer in this description. Explain it as fully as you can by saying what it suggests to you and say how it helps you to picture clearly the cloudless sky.
2 What is meant by the word 'gurgling'? With what sort of people and what particular actions do you usually associate this word? What does it suggest to you about the spring in the rocks?
3 What does this word suggest to you about the heat of the morning? The word 'advanced' is often used to describe the actions of an army on the march. How does this help you to picture the description of the scene?
4 Explain fully what the bullocks and lizards are doing. How does the switch to describing the actions of other living creatures, apart from the children and their ponies, help you to understand the extreme heat of the day?
5 Explain in your own words why the children are perspiring so heavily. What effect does the writer produce by referring to the sound made by the crane? Why do you think he uses the words 'trumpeted' and 'desperately' to describe it?
6 Now read through the final paragraph carefully. Quote and comment on words and phrases contained in it that are used to give the impression that Exeter Rocks is a peaceful and secure place. What are the features that you think might lead to its being 'a famous place'? As mentioned in the introduction to this passage, a hurricane will shortly occur; can you find any suggestions in both this paragraph and the passage as a whole, that something unexpected and highly dangerous is about to happen?

Writing imaginatively: fiction

Writing stories can be one of the most enjoyable forms of writing that you can undertake. However, writing a successful story requires a lot of thought and planning – you need to consider exactly how your original idea will develop and how it will end. As well as this, you need to establish the main character(s) and the setting of the story clearly and convincingly from the very beginning – at all times it is important to keep your readers in mind and to keep asking yourself whether what you have written will make sense to them. You will find that writing a short story involves a lot of work and this is one reason why it is not always a good idea to try to write a story when you have a limited time to do so, such as when you are taking part in an examination!

The story that follows has been included here for you to read and enjoy and as an example of how an experienced writer can involve her readers by quickly establishing the situation and characters from the very beginning. As you read through it, think about the way in which it is structured and how the writer does not over-complicate or confuse matters by including too many details or plot developments. Note that the story is written by an American writer and is set there.

THERE IS A GHOST IN MY CLOSET

By Deb Brainard

There is a ghost in my closet. Should I tell my Mom and Dad? No, they wouldn't believe me. I told them about the monsters under my bed and they said there were no monsters under my bed. But I knew they were there. They would just leave whenever Mom or Dad would show up.

The first night I saw my ghost in my closet I was scared, but I knew I couldn't wake up Mom and Dad, they would just get mad at me, so I decided to talk to my ghost in my closet. My ghost looks like my Grandmother, Nellie.

I had only met her once when I was 4 years old. I am now 8 and I can still remember it. I remember Grandma's homemade bread and pie and how the smell of them was all through the house; it was so nice and made you feel all warm inside.

Grandma was a short woman about 5 feet. She had salt and pepper hair and she wore it in a bun at all times. She also had this flowery, ruffle apron on. Grandma loved to cook and she was a good cook. Everyone loved to eat her cooking. And she always wore red lipstick too.

I asked my ghost, 'Are you Grandma Nellie?' and she just stared at me with a blank stare. So I woke up my sister Nikki who shared a room with me and asked her if she could see the ghost in the closet. She said she could and asked the ghost if she was Grandma Nellie. At first the ghost just stared at us blankly and then answered us, 'Yes, I am Grandma Nellie. I was surprised that you could see me.' She was looking at us with a smile now and she spoke very softly. She said she was here to look after us as long as we needed her. I said that I hear lots of noises outside my window at night and is that ghosts too? She said, no, that it was different animals, woodchucks, cats and bats, and there was no need to be afraid. I asked Grandma, how long would she be in our closet, and she said for as long as she feels she is needed.

Well, we spent many nights talking with Grandma. She told us how to make homemade bread and cherry pie and how to crochet. We had tea parties together and sang songs with her. She told us stories of her life, and sang to us until we went to sleep. We just loved having Grandma in the closet.

Grandma had a beautiful voice, we loved hearing her sing, and she spoke so softly and was so gentle. One night we had fallen asleep listening to Grandma singing and it seemed we had been asleep for a long time when she woke Nikki and me up.

'Missy, Missy get up!'

I woke up. 'What, Grandma?'

'Get Nikki and Billy and wake up your Mom and Dad and leave the door open and I will get your cat and dog out. You must go, go now.'

'Why?'

'The back porch is on fire! Go get out, go now.'

So I did. I woke up Mom and Dad, and Nikki grabbed Billy, and we went to the tree we were told to go to if there was a fire. Mom and Dad joined us and asked us how we knew there was a fire in the house. We said that Grandma Nellie told us. And true to her word, she had Sassy our cat and Rip our dog at the tree with us. Dad was a volunteer fireman, and we lived right across from the fire barn, so he went in and got the fire truck and set off the alarm for more help to come. They managed to put the fire out and save the house.

We lived with my Mom's Mom and Dad, Grandma Evelyn and Grandpa Wayne, for a few months before we moved back into the house.

We didn't see Grandma Nellie much after that. But we were sure glad we had a ghost in our closet and that it was Grandma Nellie.

From *www.storystar.com*

Practice tasks: writing imaginatively

> 1 Write the opening paragraphs of a mystery or ghost story. You should concentrate on describing the setting for your story, for example, the place where it is set (for instance a building, the countryside or a town), time of day or night, weather conditions and one mysterious character. You should not attempt to write a complete story but simply try to create a suitably intriguing atmosphere.
>
> 2 'The Misfit'. Write a story about someone who does not fit in with the society around him/her. You should concentrate on describing the person in order to bring him/her to life. You should try not to make the story itself too complicated.

Planning your writing

Structuring a piece of writing

The way in which you structure a piece of writing depends on the purpose of the piece and the audience it is being written for.

A structure is likely to go wrong if you don't plan the whole piece of writing before you start. Most importantly, you must know what the end is going to be. If you are writing an argumentative or informative piece, you need to be clear how you are going to balance the argument with points for and against, or how you are going to give one piece of information more prominence than another. If you are writing an imaginative piece, you need to know how you are going to introduce characters and how you are going to describe them, how you are going to create atmosphere and setting, how the plot is going to develop and how your ending is going to work.

On page 107 you will find some comments about paragraphing. Paragraphing is always important but the way you use paragraphs depends on the purpose of your writing. For instance, an informative piece will normally be divided into paragraphs of roughly equal length, as it needs to have a clear and balanced structure. In an imaginative or descriptive piece the length of the paragraphs will probably be more varied, as the different elements of the narrative will have different degrees of importance.

Generally speaking, the structure should always have the following three parts.

1 Introduction: in a factual piece, this should state briefly what the subject of the piece is and – if appropriate – what opinion you are putting forward on this topic. In an imaginative piece, you may choose to set the scene or to go for a more dramatic/immediate start.
2 Main body of explanation/argument/narrative.
3 Conclusion/story ending.

Practical ways to plan your writing

When writing under examination conditions many students are so concerned about finishing in time that it is quite obvious they do not plan their writing. This matters, because well-planned writing will almost always score more highly than writing that has not been planned. Whether you are doing a piece of writing in response to a text you have read or a piece of continuous writing for an essay or coursework assignment, it is essential that you plan what you are going to write. There are various methods you can use. **Spider diagrams** and **lists**, as explained in the following pages, are two possibilities, but you may find another method that works best for you.

Spider diagrams

Note: The essay topic used in these examples, 'A lot of our life is spent doing useless things. Is this true?' is more complex than anything that you will be set in your

Cambridge IGCSE Second Language English examination. However, the advice about planning will help you in preparing for the examination and it is likely that your teacher may ask you to write something like this as a class or coursework assignment.

Stage 1

- Write your topic in the middle of the page and around it write down all the things that you might write about.
- At this stage, don't stop to think too much – just write down any relevant ideas that come to mind.

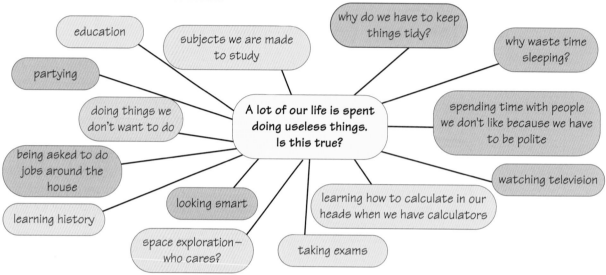

Stage 2

- The next stage is to decide if there are things that need to be discarded, and how to order the points that are being kept.
  - There are a number of points about education (linked by pink lines on the diagram below).
  - There are a number of points about personal life (linked by blue lines).
  - The idea about space exploration is probably going to be discarded.
- Number the points to give them an order; each numbered point will be a paragraph or part of a paragraph in your composition.

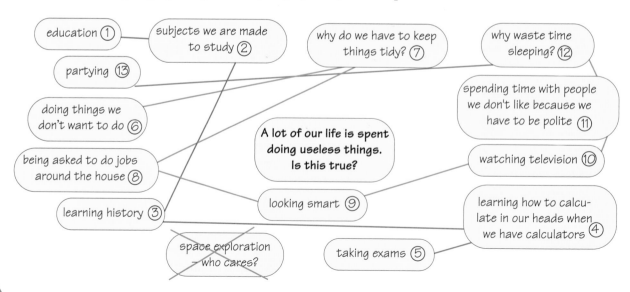

Study tip

1 At this stage, don't be afraid to cross things out.
2 If you find that two of your ideas are closely linked, you should probably combine them.
3 Remember that it is not just a case of putting forward one side of the argument – the points being made need to be answered.

Stage 3

The order of the composition now looks like this.

A lot of our life is spent doing useless things. Is this true?

Para 1   General statement about the importance of education (1)
Para 2   However – subjects we are made to study are a waste of time. (2) Why learn history? (3) Why bother to learn to do calculations in our heads – calculators! (4)
Para 3   Why do examinations in subjects which are of no importance? (5)
Para 4   General statement about doing things we don't want to do. (6)
Para 5   Being pestered to keep our rooms tidy. (7) Doing jobs around the house we don't want to. (8) Being made to look smart when we want to be comfortable. (9)
Para 6   We watch television when we can't think of anything else to do. (10) We spend time with people we don't like (perhaps relatives) because we have to. (11)
Para 7   Why can't someone invent something which means we don't have to waste time sleeping? (12) What we want to do is to party. (13)
Para 8   Conclusion What is important in life? What is unimportant?

This might not be how your plan would look in terms of content and ideas. However, it shows you how you might go about planning.

Why not take the topic title above and do your own plan? You could then go on to write the essay.

Lists

Instead of a spider diagram, you may prefer simply to put things down in a list. With this method, it's important to look carefully at the whole list again **before you start to write**.

- Don't be afraid to change the order of your points.
- Don't automatically think your first ideas are the best: check through the list and discard/replace some points if you have second thoughts.

However you choose to plan, the crucial point is this: **don't be afraid to spend time on planning!** If you have 30 minutes to do a piece of writing, you should spend 5–10 minutes planning it. One of the reasons people don't plan is because they panic about not having enough time. Look on the positive side: if you have a very clear plan in front of you, you don't have to waste time worrying about what to put next, so you will write much faster and more efficiently.

● Improving your writing

Always keep in mind the key areas that you are being assessed on for any piece of writing, whether it is a composition, a piece of directed writing or coursework. The Cambridge IGCSE Second Language English syllabus states that you should be able to:

- communicate clearly, accurately and appropriately
- convey information and express opinions effectively
- employ and control a variety of grammatical structures
- demonstrate knowledge and understanding of a range of appropriate vocabulary
- observe conventions of paragraphing, punctuation and spelling
- employ appropriate register/style.

Using Standard English

Languages vary. Each language differs according to the particular area where it is being spoken, and a language as widespread as English has many different variations and versions. There are two main kinds of variation:

- accents, which are simply variations in the way the language is pronounced
- dialects, which are more significant variations, each with its own words and expressions.

The accent and dialect spoken in an area are often an important part of that area's identity. It is a mistake to say that any particular dialect of a language is 'wrong' although, in practice, people compare other dialects of English to the form that has come to be known as Standard English.

'Standard English' is the form of English that is agreed to be generally accepted for written English, and it is the form of the language taught to students learning English. Your written work for any examination testing your English skills should therefore be almost entirely Standard English. This means following some generally recognised Standard English rules about:

- spelling (although US spelling is not penalised in some international examinations)
- punctuation
- paragraphing
- sentence structure.

While written English – for learning purposes, at least – should conform to Standard English, the same does not apply to speech. It would be impossible, for example, to speak in complete sentences all the time – and where are the paragraphs? In speech, language is much less planned and more natural. So, when you are writing in an English examination, don't write as you speak *unless* you are writing some words that were spoken or are meant to be spoken, for example:

- when you are quoting someone
- when you are writing direct speech
- when you are writing a script.

Spelling

Some people not only convince themselves that they can't spell but think that, because they can't spell, everything they write is a failure.

The first point to make is that spelling is not the most important thing in the world. If it is a problem for you, look at ways in which you can deal with it. Lack of confidence can make a problem seem worse than it really is. There is no such person as a perfect speller. Everyone makes mistakes from time to time. However, some key strategies can help to improve your spelling, as explained below.

How to improve your spelling

- **Look at words.** People who read a lot see words and absorb them. If you come across a word that you find difficult, pause for a moment and look at it. Look at the shape of the word. After a while you will find that you recognise the word more easily and you can automatically think of its shape.

- **Draw up a list of common words.** Some words occur more frequently in your writing than others. Draw up a list of these words and spend a few minutes each day or every other day reading the list, covering it up and practising writing the words.

- **Learn some spelling rules.** Although there are a lot of words that break rules, nevertheless you can learn rules about spelling which are helpful. 'I before E except after C' for example, helps you spell correctly a whole variety of words that have this letter combination. Find a book on spelling and look up the rules. Don't try to learn them all at once; just try to learn one or two at a time.

- **Say words out loud rather than just staring at the paper.** It won't always mean that you spell them correctly but, if you write down what you hear, the chances are that the word will be recognisable and it might jog your memory.

- **Use a dictionary to check your spelling rather than as the first step.** Don't be discouraged if you can't find the word straight away. Remember, for instance, that some words, such as 'know' and 'gnome', have silent first letters.

- **Make sure you copy out names correctly.** If you are doing a piece of directed writing and there are proper names in the stimulus material, or if you are responding to a piece of literature, there is no excuse for getting the spelling of names of people or places wrong.

- **Remember that vocabulary is more important than spelling.** Don't let uncertainty about spelling frighten you away from using challenging and interesting vocabulary. It is better to use interesting vocabulary with the occasional spelling error than to 'dumb down' your writing, using only very simple words that you know you can spell.

- **Most importantly, remember to check what you have written.** One of the things to check is your spelling. You will probably not correct everything, but increasingly you will find that you can spot your own mistakes.

Punctuation

The first question you should ask yourself when you are thinking about punctuation is, 'What is it for?' Punctuation is all about making life easier for the reader. In particular, it indicates to the reader where he or she needs to pause. There are four punctuation marks that indicate a pause and each indicates a different length of pause.

- The shortest pause is the **comma**. A comma allows you to group words within a longer sentence so that the reader can see the idea developing. If you can, read what you have written out loud. You will find that you naturally pause, and each time you do, put a comma.
- The longest pause is a **full stop**. You put full stops at the ends of sentences. They indicate that the point is complete and finished. Remember that you can't turn simple sentences into more complex ones just by using commas instead of full stops. However short the sentence, once the idea is complete you need to put a full stop.
- In some ways the **semi-colon** is the most difficult of the pause marks to use. When you are reading, look out for semi-colons to see where writers have used them. Read through this book and you will see that we have used semi-colons in several places. If you write a sentence in two balanced halves, and you want to keep the ideas of the two halves together rather than separating them into two sentences, use a semi-colon. The pause is a little longer than a comma and, by using it, you will be saying to the reader 'This is one idea which has two halves'.
- The last of the four pause marks is the **colon**. You use a colon most frequently to introduce a list of items. It allows a substantial pause before the list but doesn't separate everything completely, as a full stop would. (You start a list with a colon and then often use a semi-colon or a comma between the different items on the list.)

Other punctuation marks have specific jobs to do and we will mention two of them here.

- A **question mark** is a specialised full stop – in fact, part of it *is* a full stop. It is used at the end of a sentence that is in the form of a question. It is a signal to the reader that a question has been asked, and that either the next sentence will be in the form of an answer or the reader will be required to think out the answer for him- or herself.
- An **exclamation mark** is also used in place of a full stop. It is used at the ends of very short sentences, sometimes one-word sentences, where the writer wants to draw attention to something or pull the reader up short.

You must also know how to punctuate direct speech.

- You put speech marks around the words that are actually spoken.
- Other punctuation marks, such as full stops, commas and question marks, go inside the speech marks.
- Every time speech shifts from one speaker to another, you start a new line.

Remember these points and you won't go far wrong. Don't forget that the purpose of punctuation is to help the reader. Write a paragraph with no punctuation at all and see how difficult it is to read. If you read it aloud, you will notice that you naturally add the punctuation.

Using paragraphs

- A paragraph is a collection of sentences that go together to make a section of a piece of writing. The sentences are all about the same idea.
- A paragraph normally begins with a topic sentence which tells you what the paragraph is going to be about. The other sentences then develop the ideas.
- You could say that paragraphing is a sort of punctuation. A sentence is a group of words that go together to make a sensible whole; a paragraph is a group of sentences that do the same thing.

Make sure not only that you use paragraphs, but that you use them correctly. Sometimes it's easy to forget about paragraphing when you are writing quickly in the examination and concentrating on what you want to say. It's important to read through your work to make sure that:

- you have started a new paragraph often enough
- you have started the new paragraphs in sensible places.

Example of clear paragraphing

The short article which follows on pages 108–109 is written in nine paragraphs. You will see that each paragraph or group of paragraphs develops a different point.

Elsewhere we have talked about structure. Clearly the paragraphing has given this short article a very good structure.

Study tip

If the piece you are writing is for a leaflet, advert or pamphlet, or is some other kind of publicity material, you will need to use other devices as well as, or instead of, paragraphs to divide your text into 'bite-sized' chunks that are quick and easy to follow. For example, you might use:

- several short sub-headings, or
- bullet points, like the ones being used here!

Wheelchair rugby, popularly known as 'murderball', is one of the most exciting events of the Paralympic Games. The passage which follows is an extract from an article about this sport and focuses on Kylie Grimes, the only female member of the UK Team in the 2012 Games.

Murderball: Spiked wheelchairs. Crashes galore.

By David Jones

The one-sentence opening paragraph clearly establishes the point of the article and instantly engages the readers.

The second and third paragraphs supply precise details as to the cause of Kylie's disability and its results; the final sentence of the third paragraph provides a link to the more positive picture presented by the rest of the article.

Paragraphs 4 and 5 provide a summary of Kylie's career up to the present day when she is about to compete in the 2012 Paralympic Games.

Among all the uplifting biographies in these Games, Kylie's is particularly inspirational.

Aged 18, she was a sporty student who travelled the country competing in equestrian events. Then, one night, while attending a party at a friend's home, she dived into the shallow indoor swimming pool — and her life changed in an instant. Striking her head on the bottom, she snapped her spine and was paralysed from the neck down. Even her arm movements are limited, and it seemed unlikely she would ever participate in sport again.

She at first made an attempt to sue the owner of the house where the party was held for £6 million compensation, claiming there should have been a warning sign beside the pool, but she lost the case. Nevertheless, by that time, her fortunes had undergone an astonishing transformation that no money could buy.

It came when, having attempted wheelchair racing and found it too painful to sit in the required position, her therapists at the Aspire Centre for spinal injuries in Stanmore, Middlesex, suggested she try 'murderball', in which the chair is designed differently.

She started by playing for Kent Crusaders, one of just ten teams in the UK, and showed such tactical awareness and raw courage as a defensive player that within only two years she was selected for the Paralympic squad.

Wheelchair rugby is practised in over twenty countries around the world.

Paragraphs 6–8 consist of a series of comments about her daughter's strengths from Kylie's mother. This provides a wider perspective on her situation and also gives a more personal tone to the article. The very short Paragraph 8 effectively emphasises Kylie's determination and commitment to her sport.

The final paragraph returns to the writer's perspective and the situation in general, but also includes specific details about Kylie's appearance which leaves the readers with a strong sense of her individuality.

'Kylie was hooked on the sport as soon as she saw it,' says her mother, Karen. 'She has always been a great team-player, and from the moment she was injured she never looked back, only forward. She told me: "Mum, it's not about what I can't do — it's about what I can do."'

'At first I was nervous when I watched her, and she was sometimes thrown out of her chair. But now I don't worry because, as she says, she has already broken her neck — so there's not much worse that can happen, is there?'

'She knows she'll be hit just as hard as the men, and she wouldn't have it any other way.'

Having watched her yesterday, I have no doubt of it. Kylie is also clearly something of an exhibitionist — she has dyed her hair bright red for the Paralympics and had a Union Jack etched into a shaven section of her scalp.

From the *Daily Mail*, 5 September 2012

Tenses

Quite often students get tenses confused, swapping from present tense to past tense and back again, especially in stories. When you are writing, think carefully about the tense you are writing in – if you are writing in the present tense, then stick to it. You might want to flash back occasionally to remind your reader of something in the past, but make sure that you come back to the present after the flashback. If you are writing in the past, then stick with the past tense.

Controlling and choosing language

Your ability to control and choose how you use language is also important. You can demonstrate your ability by:

- using a variety of sentence structures to produce different effects
- using a variety of vocabulary which is appropriate for what you are writing.

In an examination, you will also need to show evidence of your ability to:

- structure/organise a piece of writing
- write a letter
- write informatively.

The evidence for this will often be in the way you organise and develop your writing.

Last but not least …

Make sure your handwriting can be read easily. If only one word in three is clearly legible, the reader will gain only a partial understanding of what you are trying to say. Try to see it from the reader's point of view – the person marking your examination paper can only award marks for what he or she can read!

Study tip

If you are the sort of person whose brain works faster than your pen, then when writing an examination task it may be a good idea to concentrate on writing neatly. The effort involved in doing this helps to slow down your thought processes, giving you time to organise and express your ideas clearly.

Note: Further, more detailed information about English usage (grammar, punctuation, spelling and so on) can be found in the Appendix (pages 122–43) along with exercises to help your understanding.

6 Listening and speaking skills

Assessment in oral work (speaking skills) is a compulsory element of many English examination syllabuses, including Cambridge IGCSE Second Language English. However, as well as being tested in your examination, speaking and listening are bound to be an integral part of your English lessons, and being able to speak in English and understand what is said to you in reply are hugely important skills. It's also worth remembering that if you write a script for your written papers, you will produce a better piece if you have thought about how to speak interestingly and communicate clearly.

In Chapter 5 we looked at the skills involved in writing for different purposes and for different audiences. Similar skills are needed for speaking. If you are a high court judge about to sentence someone to ten years in jail, you are going to speak rather differently from someone who is talking to a group of friends about whether to go to the cinema or to go shopping. Even in school, you adapt your speaking style to different situations – perhaps without really thinking about it: you are bound to find yourself in a mix of formal and informal situations, talking with adults and with your peers, talking about school work and your leisure time, and so on.

The following pages refer specifically to the Cambridge IGCSE Second Language English syllabus, but much of the advice and suggested tasks are appropriate for any examination syllabus that tests speaking and listening skills. In Cambridge IGCSE Second Language English both your listening and speaking skills will be assessed as separate elements of the examination. Components 3 (Core) and 4 (Extended) are part of the external examination and test your listening skills. Component 5 (a short examination conducted within your school – as opposed to an externally set examination) and Component 6 (coursework tasks) test your ability to speak English competently. In total, listening and speaking comprise 30% of the available marks for the examination if the examination taken is the Count-in oral – 0511 (15% for each skill). However, for other syllabuses where the oral is separately endorsed, the listening paper counts for 30%.

● Assessment objectives

Before we look more closely at the format and content of these components, it is important to have a clear understanding of the assessment objectives against which you will be assessed .

Assessment objective 3: Listening

L1 identify and retrieve facts and details
L2 understand and select relevant information
L3 recognise and understand ideas, opinions and attitudes and the connections between related ideas
L4 understand what is implied but not actually stated, for example gist, relationships between speakers, speaker's purpose/intention, speaker's feelings, situation or place.

Assessment objective 4: Speaking

S1 communicate clearly, accurately and appropriately
S2 convey information and express opinions effectively
S3 employ and control a variety of grammatical structures
S4 demonstrate knowledge of a range of appropriate vocabulary

S5 engage in and influence the direction of conversation

S6 employ suitable pronunciation and stress patterns.

It is important to keep in mind that the assessment objectives contain all the criteria for achieving the highest grades in the examination – you will still be graded even if you don't fulfil them all completely.

The listening test

The disc that accompanies this book contains some exercises that you can use to practise for the listening component of the Cambridge IGCSE Second Language English examination. The following paragraphs will describe in some detail what the listening test is likely to comprise and contain some advice as to how to approach it, in order to achieve the best result of which you are capable.

You are not permitted to use dictionaries for either the Core or Extended paper.

At Core level, Paper 3 lasts for about 30–40 minutes and consists of seven questions in total.

- Questions 1–4 are based on four short recorded extracts of people speaking – for example, snippets of a conversation/dialogue or in the form of something like an answer phone or voice mail message. There will be two short questions on each extract (requiring answers of no more than two or three words each) and you will be played each extract twice.

- Question 5 requires you to fill in gaps in a form or some similar form of writing that is printed on the question paper. You will be played a recording of a short talk (that you will hear twice) and then asked to fill in the gaps on the piece of writing using appropriate information given in the talk. In total, 8 marks are available for this section of the paper.
- Question 6 (which is worth 6 marks in total) requires listening to a recording of six people giving their opinions on a topic; you will then be required to match statements printed on the exam paper with the speakers who expressed the particular views. There will be seven statements to choose from, so remember that one of them will not be relevant. Again, the recording will be played twice.

- Question 7 (8 marks in total) is based on a recording of a discussion between two speakers plus a host who introduces the discussion. You will be required to answer eight multiple-choice questions (each with three options) which test your understanding of what was said in the discussion. As with the other tasks, the recording will be played twice.

At Extended level, Paper 4 lasts for about 45 minutes and consists of eight questions in total.

- Questions 1–7 are the same as the equivalent questions for the Core paper.
- Question 8 is worth 10 marks in total. You will be required to listen to a recording of a talk and then to complete some short notes on the content of this talk. The notes may be in the form of bullet points or filling in gaps in a notebook, for example. The second part of this question involves listening to a short discussion relating to the talk and then showing understanding of what was discussed by answering some short sentence completion tasks.
- All recordings will be played through twice.

● Preparing for the test

As with other elements of your English examination, it is not possible to revise for your listening paper in the same way that you might do for a subject such as geography, for example. It is, therefore, especially important that you train yourself to practise the skills required throughout the years leading up to your Cambridge IGCSE examinations.

Fortunately, listening is something that you are required to do in every school lesson that you attend so you will have had plenty of experience practising this activity. However, it is very important that you don't take your ability to listen to what is being said for granted. We have deliberately used the word **activity** earlier in this paragraph as, in order to do well in your Cambridge IGCSE listening examination, you must listen **actively**. This means that you should concentrate fully on what is being said by the people on the recording and not let your mind wander. (You may find it helps to close your eyes or to make sure that you focus them on a fixed point – the sheet of paper in front of you, for example – so that you are not distracted by what other people in the room are doing.) Remember that what you are being tested on is your ability to **identify** and **select** key facts relating to the subject matter of the recording to which you are listening.

Remember – the examination will require you to apply your **reading** skills as well as your listening ones, as it will be necessary to read the material on the question paper as well as hearing what is being said on the recording. In order to gain a good grade in the examination you must ensure that you understand clearly exactly what each question is asking for, as well as concentrating closely on the precise detail of the talk that will provide the answer to that question.

Many of the questions in the listening examination will require straightforward retrieval of facts and details contained in the talks. However, as most questions are worth only one mark you must ensure that you have selected exactly the right detail to answer each question. Again, this is a skill that you are likely to be practising in all the lessons you attend – teachers talk and give information about their particular subject and you, as the student, will be taking notes of what they say and selecting and identifying the important points that they are making. You may even find that if you view every lesson as an opportunity to prepare for your English listening examination, your performance in all of your school subjects will benefit!

There is one final point to note: assessment objective L4 refers to the need to 'understand what is implied but not actually stated'. The ability to show that you are capable of doing this is likely to be one of the requirements for a top grade mark. Understanding what is implied will not be something that you need to do for some of the more straightforward recorded passages, but you should always be alert to the fact that, in some cases, the speakers can suggest an attitude about a topic by the way they emphasise or pronounce certain words and even by the pauses they make at key points when they are talking. Again this is something that you can train yourself to do by giving close attention to what your teachers say and how they say it. You can also practise this skill by listening to speakers on the radio or television as part of your preparation for the examination.

● Speaking assessment

Your speaking skills will be assessed either by a speaking test (Component 5) or through coursework (Component 6).

The speaking test will take place at some point before the main examination period and will be conducted in your school/college by an examiner who will be a member of the school's English department or an external examiner. In total the test will last for about 15 minutes. You will be given a speaking test card which suggests a topic for the discussion you will have with the teacher/examiner. (The school will have been sent a number of these cards containing different suggested topics, so not every candidate in the Centre will talk about the same thing.)

- When you first arrive for the examination, you will be able to take part in a short 'warm-up' conversation with the teacher/examiner – this will not form part of the final assessment.
- Once the teacher/examiner has given you your topic card, you will be given two to three minutes to read through the card and to think about what you might say about the topic. You are not allowed to make any notes or to use dictionaries.
- When you have had a chance to think about the topic, the conversation/discussion with the teacher/examiner will begin. This will last for about six to nine minutes and this is what you will be assessed on.

- Your test will be recorded by the teacher/examiner, as your Centre must send samples of the tests to the Examination Board so they can be externally moderated.

In your speaking test you will be judged on the structure of your conversation, the range and appropriateness of the vocabulary that you use and how well and fluently you develop your ideas. The conversation must be entirely in English.

- To achieve a top grade in the test, you should demonstrate that you are clearly and consistently in control of the structures of your speech and that your vocabulary is sufficiently wide, varied and precise to be able to accurately convey shades of meaning and to express some quite complex ideas.
- In addition it is important for you to sustain and develop the conversation at some length and to engage fully with the teacher/examiner by being able to respond to any changes in direction that he/she may introduce into the conversation. Your pronunciation should be clear and accurate.

The points made in the previous two bullets describe the performance expected from top-grade candidates and indicate what you should be aiming towards. However, candidates with more limited English speaking skills will still score some marks and achieve a grade in this component of the examination if: they think carefully about what they want to say; express it as clearly as they can within the vocabulary range of which they are confident; and ensure that they listen carefully to and respond relevantly to the points made by the teacher/examiner.

Remember that this is a timed examination; do not be too worried if the teacher/examiner calls a halt to the test just as you think the conversation is becoming really interesting – it is important that all candidates are allowed equal time!

Preparing for the test

This section contains some ideas as to the sort of topics that could feature on the test cards. One way of preparing for the examination would be to follow the advice provided and to practise discussing the topics with a friend or family member.

The discussion

The discussion in your speaking test will take the form of a conversation with the teacher/examiner about the topic on the test card. The teacher/examiner will not take an aggressive stance but will encourage you to expand positively on the ideas you suggest. In order to make the best impression, it is important to use the preparation time to think carefully about the topic. It is important that you pay careful attention to any questions that you are asked by the teacher/examiner: your **listening** skills are important as well as your speaking ones!

The conversation should last about six to nine minutes and the comments made by the teacher/examiner will allow you to express yourself as fully and as fluently as you can.

Some suggested topics for practice

The topic of the conversation will be given to you on the test card, so you will not have had the opportunity to prepare for it in advance of the examination. However, you can be confident that the topics on the cards will have been carefully chosen to ensure that they are suitable for students of your age group and that they will allow you and your classmates sufficient opportunity to develop your ideas fully on the subject, assisted by some prompting from the teacher/examiner if required.

The topics suggested below reflect the sort of subject matter that might appear on the test cards and, as suggested earlier, will provide you with something to practise with when you prepare for the examination. Remember: these topics are for practice – there are suggestions for thinking about what you might say and how you might approach the topics. Although it is unlikely that you will have the time to prepare your points in the same detail when you are taking the actual test (when you have only two or three minutes to do so) doing so in practice should make it much easier for you to focus your ideas quickly under examination conditions.

Do you have a hobby?

You might collect stamps; you might go ballroom dancing every week; you might breed fish; you might have a pet boa constrictor which has to be fed on small live rodents; you might knit socks. The point about a hobby is that presumably it is something you enjoy and find interesting. You should be able to interest other people in it. By way of preparation, ask yourself the following questions.

- Why did I start this hobby?
- When did I start?
- How much time do I spend on my hobby?
- Why do I enjoy it?
- How else might I make my hobby interesting for the teacher/examiner?

Then you can think about how to begin your part of the conversation. You might do it in such a way that there are some obvious questions for the teacher/examiner to ask as the discussion develops.

Do you travel much?

Many of you might be lucky enough to have travelled widely; you may have been to places that you have loved; you may have been to places that you have hated. Either way, you should be able to talk about them in an interesting way. Again, you need to think about what you might say, and the following points might help.

- Think of all the places that you have visited.
- Group similar places together.
- Pick out the places that you most liked.
- Pick out those places that you didn't like at all.
- Consider what was most important to you when thinking about a place – the people, the buildings, the scenery?
- If you were to pick your favourite place, which would it be?

What do you want to do as a career?

You may have a very clear idea about what you want to do as a future career, or you may have a part-time job that will provide you with material for your discussion. Do you babysit, work in a local shop, run your own website service? Some of you might be hoping that your part-time job will expand into a future career; for others it may just be a means of earning enough money to be able to go out with friends at the weekend.

Some of you might have been sent on work experience by your school. Again, through work experience you might have discovered your future career path. Alternatively, you might have been very bored or you might have hated every moment of your experience. Even so, you will have learned something for the future.

a school newspaper

your headteacher

a member of your local community council

However you have gained your experience, whatever your ideas, ask yourself the following questions.

- Do I know what I want to do as a career?
- How did I get this idea?
- Was I influenced by others rather than making up my own mind? (For instance, do you want to do the same job as one of your parents?)
- Why am I sure I will enjoy this job?
- How important is the salary to me?
- Do I think it will be a job for life?

Are you passionate about a particular issue?

'I am a vegetarian! No one should eat meat. It is unnecessary and barbaric.'

'Animals should not be used to test products for us humans. The plight of animals that are used to test cosmetics is disgraceful. Even testing medicines on animals should not happen; use human volunteers.'

'All rubbish should be recycled. We are destroying our own planet with our pollution. People who abuse our planet should be fined huge amounts. We have to think of our children and grandchildren.'

'They are my favourite pop group. I would go to the ends of the earth to see them. Their last record was the most exciting thing I have ever heard. I know some people disagree with me but they simply don't have any soul.'

'School uniform should go!'

If you are asked to talk about an issue that you feel passionate about, you must be able to talk without being overdramatic and you must have clear reasons to use to convince your listener. If you start off by advocating that all school uniforms should be burnt and the teacher/examiner argues against you, you will not do very well if all you can do is keep repeating 'I hate it!' So decide:

- What is my subject?
- Why do I feel strongly about it?
- What do I need to say to make sure the listener understands the subject?
- What are likely to be the arguments on the other side and how will I answer them?

Is your family interesting?

It is perfectly possible that your aunt is an astronaut. Your father might have been an Olympic athlete. Your grandmother was possibly the first woman to sail around the world single-handed. Your brother might be the world pie-eating champion. In other words, there might be members of your family who have achieved outstanding success. If so, there is little doubt that you could talk about them in a fascinating way.

However, you might believe your family to be interesting for far more simple reasons. Perhaps you have lived in a variety of countries and have had to adapt to frequent moves. Perhaps you come from a very large family who are involved in a wide range of activities, which means that your family life is a non-stop whirlwind.

Before you start discussing this topic, you must decide on your way into it.

- Who or what am I going to talk about?
- Would others find the person I am going to talk about interesting?
- Are there things which I should keep private?
- If the teacher/examiner asks me a question I don't want to answer, how am I going to get out of it? (There is no problem with politely declining to answer a question and moving on.)

Have you been fascinated by a book you have read, or a play or film you have seen?

If you were given this topic, you would find it quite straightforward because the first thing you would have to do is make sure that the teacher/examiner understood what you were talking about. You would have to reiterate the plot of a novel, however briefly; you would have to tell the story of a film or a play and say who was in it, and perhaps why their performances were so good.

You may well find that you have to take the lead more than with some of the other topics. One point remains central, though; you must not only be able to tell the teacher/examiner what the book, film or play was about, but you must also be able to explain, perhaps in some detail, why it was so special for you.

Does a particular person interest you?

A wide-open topic if ever there was one, and many of the points and ideas above would lead you in. Your person might be a member of your family, it might be a singer or an actor. It might be someone from history who fascinates you.

- Choose your person.
- Make sure you know about them in detail and can interest a listener.

Study tip

Remember that the discussion will develop from the way you interpret the topic on the test card. The teacher/examiner will listen very carefully to what you say and he or she may also have some ideas of his or her own and will want to see what you think of them. In order to respond well, you need to:

- listen very carefully
- take your time in answering thoughtfully.

● Speaking coursework

Rather than entering you for the speaking test, your teachers may decide to assess your speaking skills by the coursework option. Although this involves a different method of assessment from the speaking test, the criteria on which you will be assessed are exactly the same.

Coursework assessments can take place at any time during the year leading up to the final examination period. The assessments will be introduced and conducted by your teacher and, at the end of the course, your teacher will submit your performance in three of the coursework speaking tasks for the final assessment. (It is quite possible that you will have completed more than three tasks throughout the course so that your teacher can select the best three.) Some or all of the tasks will be recorded as a sample must be sent to the Examination Board for external moderation.

The speaking tasks will be based on a variety of activities, including role play, interviews, group discussions, debates and telephone conversations. However, it is likely that you will have the opportunity to engage in other activities as well, especially if your class consists of both First and Second Language Cambridge IGCSE English candidates, as it is likely that teachers will need to run assessments for both groups at the same time. The advice and suggestions contained in the following pages are suitable for both First and Second Language candidates.

Study tip

To build your confidence in speaking, record some practice pieces. You could start by reading something out loud, just to get used to the sound of your own voice on the recording. Once you have done this, make your practice as close to the situation you will face in the test as possible – in other words, find a willing partner, do some preparation and then have a go! If you manage to do this a few times then you will feel much more confident when it comes to the test itself.

Coursework

If your school has decided to assess your speaking and listening skills by coursework, you will be assessed by your teacher three times during the course in three different speaking and listening tasks. These will involve a range of activities, most of which will involve you and at least one other person. Suggested activities are listed below, although your teacher may also suggest other equally suitable topics, such as an individual activity in which you talk about a topic that is interesting or important to you.

Possible activities

- **Role-play situations.** These could be based on a book that you are studying. For example, you may be asked to imagine that you are a character who has to make an important decision and are put in the situation where you have to explain the options open to you with other characters from the book.
- **Interviews.** These are really another form of role play and are likely to be based on real-life situations. You could be put in the position of someone who is applying for a particular job or position (for example an interview for a place at university). On the other hand, you might be asked to take the role of the person conducting the interview, not the interviewee.

- **Telephone conversations.** You will be given a particular topic for the telephone conversation. For example, you could be a customer making a call to a shop about an item that you bought recently that isn't functioning properly. Alternatively, you might be asked to play the role of the member of staff who answers the call. This type of activity requires a particular type of speaking skill, as the person to whom you are talking can respond only to what you say and how you say it as they are not able to see you and the gestures that you might make.
- **Paired or group discussions.** In which you and a partner or partners (either classmates and/or the teacher) take part in a role play or an interview about a topic of interest, for example an argument between neighbours or a mock interview for a position of importance within the community.
- **Debates.** In which you are part of a small group of students who are involved in a discussion relating to a particular scenario. For example, a panel of experts discussing the performance of a local sports team in an important game.

The suggestions given for practice topics on pages 115–19 could equally form the basis of an individual activity if the teacher offers you the opportunity to do this.

What is certain is that your teacher will want to give you the opportunity to speak and listen in a variety of contexts. It is worth thinking about the different purposes for which we need to talk. We might need to:

- explain
- describe
- narrate, read or recite
- analyse in detail
- imagine something and interest the listener in it
- put some ideas together and then explore them, either with a partner or in a group
- discuss
- argue (not in the sense of having a row but of putting forward your view)
- persuade.

Remember that it is always your job to decide why you are talking and therefore how you should speak.

Remember also that with coursework there is no need to be nervous, because if things go wrong you and your teacher can always decide that you can have another go later. But then, things won't go wrong!

How are speaking tasks marked?

For both the speaking test and coursework tasks your performance(s) will be recorded and the recording sent to a moderator who is appointed by the Examination Board. The moderator receives a number of recordings and compares them with the standards that have been set. He or she will decide whether you have been assessed at the right standard. If he or she agrees with your teacher's marks, the results will simply be sent to the Examination Board; if the moderator doesn't quite agree with your teacher then he or she might adjust your marks slightly.

Appendix: Technical skills

This chapter contains a variety of information about technical aspects of the English language, such as parts of speech, punctuation, vocabulary usage and grammar. There are also some practice exercises. We suggest that you look upon this chapter mainly as a reference section, to reinforce points that you have almost certainly covered during your earlier years of studying the English language in school.

● Writing in sentences

- A **sentence** is a group of words making a complete unit of sense; it contains a **finite verb** and a **subject** of this verb; all sentences contain at least one **main clause**. For example: 'You turn left at the crossroads.' A sentence that contains just one statement like this one is called a **simple sentence**. Some sentences, however, consist of two main ideas, joined by a **conjunction**, for example: 'You turn left at the crossroads *and* then carry on for another 100 metres.' This type of sentence is known as a **compound sentence**. Finally, some sentences contain a mixture of main and **subordinate clauses**. A subordinate clause, such as that indicated in italics in the example that follows, is a group of words, containing a verb, which is dependent on the main clause for its full meaning to be clear. For example: 'You turn left at the crossroads and then carry on down for another 100 metres where you will find a signpost directing you to the bus station *which is in Garden Square facing the post office.*' This is known as a **complex sentence**.
- A sentence starts with a **capital letter**. The end of a sentence is indicated by a **full stop** (or a **question mark** or **exclamation mark**). For example: 'You turn left at the crossroads. The crossroads are very busy so you should watch the traffic carefully.' There are two distinct statements made in this piece of writing. Each has a different subject and each contains a main clause with a finite verb. The only punctuation stop which has sufficient force to separate two such distinct statements is a full stop.

> **Study tip**
>
> One of the most common errors made by examination candidates in their writing is to use a comma to separate sentences when a full stop, question mark or exclamation mark must be used.

- Most skilful writers will use a mixture of all three sentence types in their work and, in order to achieve good marks for the writing tasks in an examination, it is important to show that you, too, can confidently vary your sentence structure. However, remember that complex sentences are most effective for conveying involved and complicated ideas. When you are writing something which is intended to convey straightforward information or instructions, it is best not to over-complicate your sentence structure.

● Paragraphs

- A **paragraph** is a collection of sentences, all related to the same point, in which the key idea of the paragraph is explored and developed.
- Whatever type of writing you are producing, it is important that you pay careful attention to your use of paragraphs. These will provide the backbone of structure necessary to make what you say clearly understood by the reader.

- Each paragraph should contain a **topic sentence** which expresses the main point of the paragraph; the rest of the paragraph should develop and expand on this idea. The topic sentence can come at any point in a paragraph, depending on the effect you want to achieve.
- Each paragraph should develop from the one preceding it and link naturally into the one that follows, so that your writing shows a logical progression from one point to the next.
- When planning a piece of informative or instructional writing, it is a good idea to do so by thinking of the topic sentences which will underlie your paragraphs, and then organising them in the most logical order, before you produce your final draft.

Sentence exercises

1 Rewrite the following, inserting capital letters and full stops as necessary.
   a) The teacher walked quietly into the room the boy at the front of the room did not notice and continued with his imitation of the teacher's way of speaking the rest of the class went silent
   b) I really think that it is a good idea to read the instruction booklet on how to wire up this piece of electrical equipment before you turn it on you might have a nasty accident if you don't do so
   c) This is the fastest car in its price bracket that you can buy it accelerates from 0–60 in five seconds you will find it very exciting to drive
   d) A holiday in the Caribbean will give you the experience of a life-time the beaches are fantastic you will meet the friendliest people on earth the food is delicious and original
   e) My grandmother was a very happy woman she lived in the country all her life she never had very much money she lived a simple life her garden and small farm provided her with all the food she needed

2 Turn each of the following groups of simple sentences into one complex sentence, using any method you think suitable.
   a) Maria was feeling bored. She had been on holiday for three days. It had been raining all week. She decided that she must get out of the house.
   b) Maria picked up the telephone. She dialled the number of her friend, Consuela. Consuela answered in a sleepy and tired voice.
   c) Consuela was pleased when she heard Maria's voice. She had been very depressed by the bad weather. Now there might be a chance to do something interesting.
   d) Maria suggested that they went into town. Her older brother was at home. She would ask him if he would drive them in his car. They would call for Consuela in thirty minutes.
   e) Consuela put down the telephone. She was very pleased with Maria's suggestion. She ran into her bedroom. She needed to get ready quickly. She also wanted to eat some breakfast.

Paragraph exercises

Here are five topic sentences. Use each of them as the basis for a single paragraph of your own. Remember that all ideas in each paragraph must relate to the topic sentence. You should try to vary the position of the topic sentences so that not all of them are used at the beginning of a paragraph.

a) He mounted his bicycle and rode quickly away.
b) These are the reasons why I particularly enjoy visiting my grandmother.
c) It had been raining heavily without stopping for five days.
d) The Principal sat back in his comfortable chair and thought that the day had turned out better than he had feared.
e) These are the main reasons why _____ is my favourite movie star.

(*Fill in the blank with your favourite's name.*)

● Punctuation: commas

Commas are an important punctuation device. However, it is very easy to misuse them. They should be used only for specific purposes. The following list explains the main occasions when commas should be used. You'll notice that six of these uses are purely mechanical, while the other two require a little more care.

1 To separate words (especially adjectives) or phrases in a list or series (except for the last two words, which are usually joined by 'and').

   For example: 'Mr Anderson was a mean, cruel, bad-tempered, miserly and thoroughly unpleasant young man.'

2 To mark off the name or title of a person being addressed.

   For example: 'Mr Anderson, you've just dropped your wallet.' Or 'Excuse me, Mr Anderson, could you please give me my money back?'

3 To mark off words or phrases in apposition (that is, words which are parallel in meaning to others in the same sentence.)

   For example: 'Mr Anderson, the shopkeeper, is a very rich man.'

4 To mark off words and phrases which have been added into a sentence, such as however, therefore, nevertheless, moreover, on the other hand, etc.

   For example: 'Make sure, however, that when you are talking to Mr Anderson, you are always polite.'

5 To mark off phrases beginning with a participle when it is necessary to make a pause in reading.

   For example: 'Mr Anderson, seeing that my father was also a rich man, asked him if he would like to have lunch.'

6 In conjunction with speech marks to indicate the beginning of a passage of direct speech.

   For example: 'Mr Anderson rose to his feet and said, "......."'

7 To separate an adjectival clause beginning with 'who', 'whom' or 'which' from the rest of the sentence, when it is non-defining. This is a particularly tricky use of the comma, but the following example will help to explain the point.

   For example: 'Mr Anderson ordered that all the schoolchildren, who were in his shop, should be punished.'

   In this sentence, the clause 'who were in his shop' must be non-defining and, therefore, means that all the children in the school happened to be in his shop at that particular time. However, if the commas were not there, the sense would be that the Mr Anderson ordered that only the children in his shop were to be punished. (Those who were at home or still in school were lucky!)

8 To break up a sentence into smaller parts and to help the reader to grasp the meaning.

   For example: 'Mr Anderson, bad-tempered and angry, stormed into the school building, knocked on the Principal's door and then, before the Principal could ask him what he wanted, launched into a tirade about the bad behaviour of young people today.'

Punctuation exercise 1

Rewrite the following passage, inserting commas and full stops as necessary. Remember to change letters to capitals too, if needed!

Mr Da Silva the Principal of Happy Valley High School was not a happy man he had just received a communication from a very angry rich and powerful man named Mr Anderson who wanted him Mr Da Silva to punish a group of children who had been in Mr Anderson's shop after school knowing that Mr Anderson was the sort of person who would not listen to any excuses and who no matter how many times anyone tried to persuade him otherwise would never change his mind Mr Da Silva nevertheless felt that he ought to try to put in a good word for the children in his school who were he knew not really naughty just high spirited reluctantly he opened his door to Mr Anderson when he heard him approach and was just about to speak when Mr Anderson shouted 'Mr Da Silva it's time we had a talk'

● Punctuation: semi-colons and colons

These two punctuation devices should not be confused. Each has specific purposes and the ability to use them correctly and with confidence is one of the marks of a skilled writer.

Semi-colons are used for two main purposes:

● To separate two main clauses when they could otherwise be joined by a conjunction, such as 'and', 'or', 'but'.

For example: 'Banning traffic from the town centre will make life safer for pedestrians; it will also make the area much quieter.'

These two statements could also be joined by using 'and'; however, the use of the semi-colon gives the second half of the sentence equal force with the first.

● To separate clauses or phrases in a list. (Remember: single words in a list are separated by commas.)

For example: 'The government must make up their mind about what should be done: they can ban all traffic in the town centre at all times; they can ban cars and lorries using the town centre on week days only; they can allow commercial vehicles but ban private ones completely or they can leave things exactly as they are.'

Colons are used for three main purposes. These are:

● To separate two statements where the second expands on the meaning of the first.

For example: 'His heart sank as he approached the town centre: the traffic was at a complete standstill and there was no indication that it would be moving again for at least an hour.'

● To introduce a number of items or options in a list.

For example: 'The government must make up their mind about what should be done: they can ban all traffic in the town centre at all times; they can ban cars and lorries using the town centre on week days only; they can allow commercial vehicles but ban private ones completely or they can leave things exactly as they are.

● To introduce a speech or a quotation.

For example: 'Hamlet: To be or not to be, that is the question.'

Punctuation exercise 2

Rewrite the following passage inserting semi-colons and colons as necessary.

The sun was shining it was a fine day. Yousry awoke drew back the curtains in his bedroom looked happily at the glittering sea in the distance and decided that he would call his friends and suggest they spent the day at the beach. He thought about what he would have to take with him and started to pack his bag it was not particularly large so he knew that he had to think carefully. Finally he decided on the following a bottle of ice cold water his bathing costume and a towel some sandwiches for his lunch a large bottle of sun lotion his baseball cap to protect his head from the sun and a pair of sunglasses.

● Punctuation: apostrophes

Apostrophes are used for two main purposes:

1 to indicate when a letter or letters have been left out of a word (**omission**)
2 to show **possession**.

The first of these uses is quite easy to understand; the second can be more problematic.

- **Omission.** One way of giving your writing a more informal or colloquial tone is by **contracting** the form of some words.

  For example: in speech, most people would not say something like, 'I *do not* think that *we will* be able to go to the beach tomorrow. It *is not* a good day as there *will not* be any transport available.' Instead, they would use contracted forms of the words in italics.

  When you write such contracted forms, you must use apostrophes to show where letters have been left out: 'I *don't* think that *we'll* be able to go to the beach tomorrow. It *isn't* a good day as there *won't* be any transport available.'

- **Possession.** In order to show possession (that is, to show the owner of something) when there is only one person or thing concerned, an apostrophe, followed by the letter -s, is put at the end of the noun indicating the person or thing that is the possessor.

  For example:

Possessor	Possessive form
Girl	The girl's dress
Boy	The boy's book
School	The school's classrooms

- However, if there is more than one possessor (and the plural form of the noun is indicated by the letter -s) then the possessive is shown by adding an apostrophe after the -s showing the plural.

  For example:

Possessor	Possessive form
Girls	The girls' dresses
Boys	The boys' books
Schools	The schools' classrooms

Notes:

(i)   When the plural of a noun is **not** formed by adding -s, then the possessive is shown by -'s.

For example: 'The men's changing room'; 'The women's changing room'; 'The children's playground'.

(ii)   The only word which determines the position of the apostrophe is the noun indicating the possessor. Whether one person possesses many things or many people share the ownership of one thing, there is no deviation from the apostrophe rule.

For example: 'The girl's presents' (one girl owning many presents) and 'The teachers' staffroom' (many teachers, but only one room).

(iii)   The apostrophe should be used in expressions such as 'a week's holiday', 'a day's sickness', 'an hour's delay'.

(iv)   The apostrophe is only used in the word **it's** when it is a contraction for **it is**.

For example: 'It's a hot day today.'

The apostrophe is **not** used on the possessive adjective **its**.

For example: 'The dog ate its bone.'

Punctuation exercise 3

Rewrite the following sentences using apostrophes as required.

a) Katijas books were left in the schools dining room.
b) 'Whats the matter with the cat? It cant seem to find its food.'
c) 'Ive had at least a months wait for this letter; its about time something turned up.'
d) Mr Rajans car was missing a hub cap.
e) The boys football had been lost among the gardens long grass.
f) 'Whats this ball doing here? This is the Mayors private property.'
g) The birds nests were blown out of the trees by the winds force.
h) 'Where are you going? Im not going with you; its too late.'
i) Both of the History teachers cars radiators were not working properly.
j) Mrs Flemings sons house wasnt very close to his wifes place of work.

● Punctuation: dashes and hyphens

These two punctuation devices should not be confused. The **dash** is used for a variety of purposes. Its main use is to show where there is an interruption to the intended structure of a sentence, for example when an afterthought is added or an interruption occurs. In these cases, a dash is placed before and after the words that are interjected – unless the interruption occurs at the end of a sentence, when it will be concluded with the conventional device such as a full stop, question mark or exclamation mark.

For example:

● 'She offered me some of her lunch – and very tasty it was too – before we went back into lessons.'
● 'She offered me some of her lunch before we went back into lessons – and very tasty it was too!'

Another time when a dash is used is to show when a word or sentence is not completed.

For example:

- 'I'll tell you who the murderer is; it was –' a single shot silenced him before he could pronounce the name we had all been waiting for.
- The police would not tell us who the suspect was; they referred to him as Mr J–.

Another use of the dash is to indicate a sudden dramatic end to a sentence. For example:

- 'I'll tell you who committed the murder,' said the detective. 'It was – the mayor.'

A **hyphen** is not really a punctuation mark at all; it is simply a way of linking compound words together (for example, as in 'the sea was a bluish-grey colour') or as a sign that a word has been split into syllables when there is no space to fit the complete word in at the end of a line of writing, for example 'eat-ing'. In this case, it is important that you place the hyphen between syllables and not between letters at random (for example 'eati-ng').

Punctuation exercise 4

Here is an extract from a short story with all the punctuation removed. Put in the punctuation (including dashes).

it was very slowly I recovered my memory of my experience you believe now said the old man that the room is haunted he spoke no longer as one who greets an intruder but as one who grieves for a broken friend yes said i the room is haunted and you have seen it and we who have lived here all our lives have never set eyes upon it because we have never dared . . . tell us is it truly the old earl who no said i it is not i told you so said the old lady with the glass in her hand it is his poor young countess who was frightened it is not i said there is neither ghost of earl nor ghost of countess in that room there is no ghost there at all but worse far worse well they said the worst of all the things that haunt poor mortal man said i and that is in all its nakedness fear fear that will not have light nor sound that will not bear with reason that deafens and darkens and overwhelms it followed me through the corridor it fought against me in the room i stopped abruptly there was an interval of silence my hand went up to my bandages

From *The Red Room* by H.G. Wells

● Direct speech punctuation

If you are using **direct speech** in your writing, it is important that you punctuate it correctly and observe the appropriate conventions. Here are the key points to remember:

- Direct speech should be placed within either double ("...") or single ('...') **inverted commas** (**speech marks**). It does not matter which form of speech marks you choose to use, but once you have decided you must be consistent.
- All passages of direct speech must be marked off from the rest of the sentence in which they occur by a comma.
- The opening word of each piece of direct speech must begin with a capital letter.
- You should start a new line for each new speaker.

- If you quote someone else's words within a passage of direct speech, then these words must also be enclosed within speech marks. If the original piece of speech is indicated by double inverted commas, then further quotations should be placed within single inverted commas and vice versa.
- If a single piece of direct speech consists of more than one paragraph, then the opening set of inverted commas is repeated at the start of each new paragraph. However, the closing inverted commas are not used until the very end of the passage of speech.

Here are some examples of the three different patterns of direct speech and of how they should be punctuated:

1 The teacher said, "I'm very pleased with the last piece of work you did for me."
2 "Thank you, Sir," I replied, "but I found it a very difficult assignment. Will we have anything else like that in future?"
3 "I'm sure you will," answered the teacher. "You need as much practice with this topic as you can get."

In the first example, a comma is used after the introductory verb (said) and before the words actually spoken, which begin with a capital letter.

In the second example, the words 'I replied' break the direct speech and are separated from the rest of the sentence by commas. The opening word of the second part of this direct speech sentence does not have a capital letter, however, because it continues a sentence that has already begun.

In the final example, the two pieces of direct speech, separated by 'answered the teacher', are two distinct sentences. The opening word of the second sentence (You) is, therefore, given a capital letter.

Punctuation exercise 5

Punctuate the following passage, putting in paragraphs, commas, full stops, speech marks, capital letters and question marks as necessary.

the classroom was unusually quiet the principal strode to the front of the room and stood at the teacher's desk he waited for a minute before he spoke i want you all to listen very carefully he said in a quiet voice someone in here has been very rude to a visitor to the school someone shouted the word idiot at the mayor as he walked through the playground i want to know who it was brian raised his hand yes boy said the principal was it you it might have been me sir whispered brian what do you mean it might have been me surely you know if you said it or not brian looked very worried i did call out the word idiot in the playground he said but i didn't see the mayor there he must have thought i was shouting the word at him but all i was doing was shouting at myself we were playing football and i missed an open goal that's the truth sir

● Vocabulary work: homonyms, homophones and homographs

The Greek prefix 'homo-' means 'the same'. The exercises in this section are all based on groups of words that have similarities.

Homonyms are words that have the same spelling and pronunciation, but different meanings. For example, 'bit' as in a small item of something and 'bit' as the past tense of the verb 'to bite'.

Homophones are words that have the same pronunciation but a different spelling and different meanings, such as 'rain' (something wet that falls from the sky); 'rein', a device for controlling a horse and 'reign', the action performed by a king or queen in control of a country.

Homographs are words that have the same spelling but different pronunciations and meanings, such as 'close', a verb meaning to shut, and 'close', an adjective meaning near to.

Being able to distinguish between words in these different categories is an important requirement in being able to write and speak English fluently.

Exercise 1: Homonyms

The following words all have at least two different meanings. Use each word in at least two different sentences which make the meanings clear:

bear, bow, fair, lap, lean, lie, page, pen, plain, train

Exercise 2: Homophones

Use each of the following pairs of words in sentences, making clear the differences in their meanings:

allowed/aloud
ascent/assent
bare/bear
berth/birth
cereal/serial
flair/flare
freeze/frieze
higher/hire
hoarse/horse
pedal/peddle

Exercise 3: Homographs

The following words have a different meaning, depending on how they are pronounced. Write two sentences for each word to illustrate their different meanings:

bow, desert, entrance, lead, live, minute, refuse, row, wind, wound

● Spelling and vocabulary work

Some English words are spelt differently depending upon what part of speech they are. Here are some examples:

Verb	Noun
advise	advice
practise	practice
prophesy	prophecy
license	licence
affect	effect*

*Effect can also be used as a verb with the meaning 'to produce or to bring something about'.

Verbs

Verbs are words which express an action or a state of being and are central to the structure of a sentence; for example:

- 'The batsman *struck* the ball.'
- 'The sun *shone*.'
- 'The ugly duckling *became* a swan.'

In each of these examples the verb is in italics.

In the first example, the verb 'struck' is followed by the noun 'ball', which is referred to technically as the **object** of the verb. A verb which is followed by an object is called a **transitive verb**.

In the second example, there is no object in the sentence. A verb such as 'shone', which is not followed by an object, is called an **intransitive verb**.

The verb in the third example, 'became', expresses a state of being and not an action. In this sentence, the subject of the verb ('duckling') and the word following it ('swan') refer to the same thing; the word following verbs such as 'become' is referred to as the **complement** of the sentence.

A **finite** or **main verb** is a form of a verb which expresses an action or state of being which is complete in itself. It has **tense** (past, present or future) and **number** (singular or plural); for example:

- 'I ran to school.'
- 'It is a cold day.'
- 'He waits for me at the bus stop.'
- 'There are no clouds in the sky.'

All of these simple sentences make complete sense and it is the form of the verb which ensures that this is so.

A finite verb can be in either the **active** or the **passive mood**. In the active, the subject of the verb performs the action (for example: 'The batsman *struck* the ball.'), whereas if the verb is in the passive form, the subject suffers the action of the verb (for instance: 'The ball *was struck* by the batsman.')

Not all forms of the verb convey a complete meaning and, therefore, need to relate to something else in the sentence. Such forms of the verb are known as **non-finite**. The most common non-finite parts of a verb are:

- the **infinitive** ('to talk', 'to beat', etc.)
- the **present participle** ('talking', 'beating', etc.)
- the **past participle** ('talked', 'beaten', etc.).

When used in sentences, the infinitive functions as a noun; for example:

- 'He liked to eat.'

And the participles usually function as adjectives; for example:

- 'The talking parrot amused the children.'
- 'The beaten team left the ground as soon as they had changed out of their kit.'

One further non-finite part of the verb is the **gerund** or **verbal noun**. As the alternative name suggests, the gerund is a part of the verb which functions grammatically as a noun. In form it is the same as the present participle. For example, the gerund of the verb 'to dance' is 'dancing'. It can be used in a sentence as either the subject or the object of a verb. For example: 'Dancing is an activity that can be enjoyed by all ages' and 'My grandparents enjoy dancing and so do I'. Because it is a noun, it can be described by an adjective, as in 'Hip-hop dancing is a very enjoyable activity'.

Although the gerund functions as a noun, it still retains its character as a verb. In the following sentence, for example, the gerund 'banging' is both the subject of the verb 'upset' (and, therefore, doing the work of a noun) and also has its own object, 'drum', and so keeps its verbal function: 'The child's continuously banging his drum upset our concentration.'

Note: As the gerund is a noun, it must be accompanied by a possessive and not a personal pronoun (this is a common confusion and error of expression). There is a significant difference between the following sentences: 'I don't like his dancing' (in other words, it is the way he dances that is not liked, not the person himself) and 'I don't like him dancing' (this is grammatically incorrect, but if it meant anything, would mean, 'I don't like the person who happens to be dancing').

Subjunctive mood

As well as the active and passive moods, a verb can also be used in the **subjunctive mood**. This is when a verb is used to express a condition that is doubtful, not factual, or wishful. It is very often used in a sentence or clause introduced by the word 'if'.

The subjunctive mood is also used in subordinate clauses that follow verbs that express feelings such as doubt, request or wish. For example, the verbs that most commonly introduce a clause using the subjunctive are: ask, demand, determine, insist, move, order, pray, prefer, recommend, regret, request, require, suggest, and wish.

In Standard English usage there is no difference between the subjunctive and normal form of the verb apart from in the third person singular of the present tense and in the verb 'to be'. In the subjunctive mood, the normal present tense form of the third person singular (for example, he runs, she catches) loses the final -s or -es so that it takes the same form as the first and second person singular (for instance, he run, she catch).

- He recommended that she catch the earlier bus as it would be less crowded.

In this example, the verb 'catch' is in the subjunctive mood as it follows a wishful statement and contrasts with the normal (or indicative) use of the verb 'to catch' as in the sentence 'She catches the ball as it is thrown to her'.

The subjunctive form of the verb 'to be', however, is 'be' in the present tense and 'were' in the past tense for first, second and third person forms. For example:

- If I were you, I would apply for the job without any hesitation.

In this sentence, the verb 'were' is part of the statement 'if I were you', which is a non-factual condition (one person cannot actually become another), and so the subjunctive is used. However, in a sentence such as 'When I saw the advertisement, I applied straightaway for the job.' a straightforward action taking place in the past is described and so the straightforward past tense is used.

Pronouns

The term **pronoun** covers many words, and, in general, refers to words that can take the place of a noun used earlier, such as 'he', 'she' and 'they'. There are many different kinds of pronouns, however, and confusing their use can cause problems when you are trying to express yourself in English. The list below is mainly for reference purposes.

Demonstrative pronouns

These pronouns are used to demonstrate (or indicate). **This**, **that**, **these** and **those** are all demonstrative pronouns, for example:

- **This** is the one I left in the car.

In this example, the speaker could be referring to a mobile phone, for instance, in which case the pronoun 'this' replaces the words 'mobile phone'.

- Shall I take **those**?

In this example 'those' could replace, for instance, 'those apples'.

Indefinite pronouns

Unlike demonstrative pronouns, which point out specific items, indefinite pronouns are used for non-specific things. This is the largest group of pronouns. **All**, **some**, **any**, **several**, **anyone**, **nobody**, **each**, **both**, **few**, **either**, **none**, **one** and **no one** are the most common. For example:

- **Somebody** must have seen the driver leave.

  ('somebody' – not a specific person)

- We are **all** in the gutter, but **some** of us are looking at the stars. (Oscar Wilde)
- I have **nothing** to declare except my genius. (Oscar Wilde)

Interrogative pronouns

These pronouns are used in questions. Although they are classified as pronouns, it is not easy to see how they replace nouns. **Who**, **which**, **what**, **where** and **how** are all interrogative pronouns. For example:

- **Who** told you to do that?

Possessive pronouns

Possessive pronouns are used to show possession. As they are used as adjectives, they are also known as 'possessive adjectives'. **My**, **your**, **his**, **her**, **its**, **our** and **their** are all possessive pronouns. For example:

- Have you seen **her** book?

In this example, the pronoun 'her' replaces a word like 'Sarah's'.

We use possessive pronouns to refer to a specific person/people or thing/things (the 'antecedent') belonging to a person/people (and sometimes belonging to an animal/animals or thing/things).

We use possessive pronouns depending on:

- Number – **singular** (for example **mine**) or **plural** (for example **ours**)
- Person – **1st person** (for example **mine**), **2nd person** (for example **yours**) or **3rd person** (for example **his**)
- Gender – **male** (for example **his**), **female** (for example **hers**).

Below are the possessive pronouns, followed by some example sentences. Notice that each possessive pronoun can:

- be subject *or* object
- refer to a singular *or* plural antecedent.

Number	Person	Gender (of 'owner')	Possessive pronouns
singular	1st	male/female	mine
	2nd	male/female	yours
	3rd	male	his
		female	hers
		neuter	its
plural	1st	male/female	ours
	2nd	male/female	yours
	3rd	male/female/neuter	theirs

- Look at these pictures. **Mine** is the big one. (subject = My picture)
- I like your flowers. Do you like **mine**? (object = my flowers)
- I looked everywhere for your key. I found Maria's key but I couldn't find **yours**. (object = your key)
- My flowers are dying. **Yours** are lovely. (subject = Your flowers)

- All the essays were good but **his** was the best. (subject = his essay)
- Maria found her passport but John couldn't find **his**. (object = his passport)
- John found his spectacles but Maria couldn't find **hers**. (object = her spectacles)
- The hurricane damaged the house's roof but the shed completely lost **its**. (object = its roof)

- Here is your car. **Ours** is over there, where we left it. (subject = Our car)
- Your photos are good. **Ours** are terrible. (subject = Our photos)

- Each couple's books are colour-coded. **Yours** are red. (subject = Your books)
- I don't like this family's garden but I like **yours**. (object = your garden)

- These aren't John and Lee's children. **Theirs** have black hair. (subject = Their children)
- John and Lee don't like your car. Do you like **theirs**? (object = their car)

Notice that the interrogative pronoun 'whose' can also be a possessive pronoun (an interrogative possessive pronoun). Look at these examples:

- There was $100 on the table and Maria wondered **whose** it was.
- This car hasn't moved for two months. **Whose** is it?

Relative pronouns

Relative pronouns are used to add more information to a sentence. **Which, that, who** (including **whom** and **whose**) and **where** are all relative pronouns. For example:

- Dr James Montgomery, **who** lectured at the university for more than 12 years, should have known the difference.

In this example, the relative pronoun 'who' introduces the clause 'who lectured at the university for 12 years' and refers back to 'Dr James Montgomery'.

- The man **who** first saw the comet reported it as a UFO.

In this example, the relative pronoun 'who' introduces the clause 'who first saw the comet' and refers back to 'the man'.

Absolute possessive pronouns

These pronouns also show possession. Unlike possessive pronouns (see above), which are adjectives related to nouns, these pronouns are used by themselves. **Mine, yours, his, hers, ours** and **theirs** are all absolute possessive pronouns. For example:

- The tickets are as good as **ours**.
- Shall we take **yours** or **theirs**?

Reciprocal pronouns

Reciprocal pronouns are used for actions or feelings that are reciprocated. The two most common reciprocal pronouns are **each other** and **one another**. For example:

- They like **one another**.
- They talk to **each other** like they're old friends.

Reflexive pronouns

A reflexive pronoun ends -**self** or -**selves** and refers to another noun or pronoun in the sentence. The reflexive pronouns are **myself, yourself, herself, himself, itself, ourselves, yourselves** and **themselves**. For example:

- Paul bakes all the bread **himself**.

In this example, the reflexive pronoun 'himself' refers back to the noun 'Paul'.

Personal pronouns

Personal pronouns represent specific people or things. We use them depending on:

- Number – **singular** (for example **I**) or **plural** (for example **we**).
- Person – **1st person** (for example **I**), **2nd person** (for example **you**) or **3rd person** (for example **he**).

- Gender – **male** (for example **he**), **female** (for example **she**) or **neuter** (for example **it**).
- Case – **subject** (for example **we**) or **object** (for example **us**).

We use personal pronouns in place of the person or people that we are talking about. For example:

- My name is Lee but when I am talking about myself I almost always use 'I' or 'me', not 'Lee'.
- When I am talking directly to you, I almost always use 'you', not your name.
- When I am talking about another person, say John, I may start with 'John' but then use 'he' or 'him'.

Here are the personal pronouns, followed by some example sentences:

Number	Person	Gender	Personal pronouns	
			Subject	Object
singular	1st	male/female	I	me
	2nd	male/female	you	you
	3rd	male	he	him
		female	she	her
		neuter	it	it
plural	1st	male/female	we	us
	2nd	male/female	you	you
	3rd	male/female/neuter	they	them

Examples (in each case, the first example shows a **subject pronoun**, the second an **object pronoun**):

- **I** like coffee.
- Do **you** like coffee?
- **He** runs fast.
- **She** is clever.
- **It** doesn't work.
- **We** went home.
- Do **you** need a table for three?
- **They** played doubles.

- John helped **me**.
- John loves **you**.
- Did Vikram beat **him**?
- Does Raja know **her**?
- Can the engineer repair **it**?
- Mei Ling drove **us**.
- Did Lee and John beat **you** at doubles?
- Lee and John beat **them**.

When we are talking about a single thing, we almost always use **it**. However, there are a few exceptions. We may sometimes refer to an animal as **he/him** or **she/her**, especially if the animal is domesticated or a pet. Ships (and some other vessels or vehicles) as well as some countries are often treated as female and referred to as **she/her**. Here are some examples:

- This is our dog Bandit. **He**'s an Alsatian.
- The *Titanic* was a great ship but **she** sank on her first voyage.
- My first car was a Mini and I treated **her** like my wife.
- Thailand has now opened **her** border with Cambodia.

For a single person, sometimes we don't know whether to use **he** or **she**. There are several solutions to this:

- If a teacher needs help, **he or she** should see the principal.
- If a teacher needs help, **he** should see the principal.

We often use **it** to introduce a remark:

- **It** is nice to have a holiday sometimes.
- **It** is important to dress well.
- **It's** difficult to find a job.
- Is **it** normal to see them together?
- **It** didn't take long to walk here.

We also often use **it** to talk about the weather, temperature, time and distance:

- **It's** raining.
- **It** will probably be hot tomorrow.
- Is **it** nine o'clock yet?
- **It's** 50 kilometres from here to Cambridge.

Language and usage practice

In this final section we are going to focus on a selection of points to do with the use of English and, in particular, to consider some points relating to errors and misunderstandings made by candidates in examinations.

Pronouns and agreement

Just to recap on a few main points: pronouns take the place of nouns that have already been used – if you don't make use of pronouns then your expression will sound stilted and awkward. However, it's important to keep in mind that pronouns have to agree with the word they replace in number, gender and person. So, if the original noun is masculine, singular and in the third person then the pronoun that replaces it must have the same features. For example, it is correct to write 'Daniel enjoyed his fast-food meal' as the pronoun 'his' agrees with the noun 'Daniel' in all three aspects, whereas to write 'Daniel enjoyed their fast-food meal' would be incorrect (unless you mean that Daniel was eating the meal belonging to two or more other people!).

In this example, the error is easy to spot and most people would avoid making it in the first place. However, other uses of pronouns can be more tricky. Consider the following sentences:

1 All pupils must bring their sports kit to school tomorrow.
2 All the girls remembered to bring their kit.
3 No-one among the boys was in trouble for forgetting his.

Sentence 2 is correct as 'All the girls' implies that there was more than one girl involved and so the pronoun 'their' is correct. In Sentence 3, the indefinite pronoun 'No-one' is singular (as indicated by the word 'one') and is correctly followed by the singular verb 'was' and the singular personal pronoun 'his'.

Study tips

1 Indefinite pronouns such as **no-one**, **nobody**, **none**, **nothing**, **everyone**, **everybody**, **anyone** and **anybody** are all singular in meaning and usage.
2 Using the noun 'one' in a sentence also leads to pronoun errors. For example, the sentence 'One should be sure not to forget his sports kit tomorrow' is clearly incorrect; the problem lies in the fact that the only word that can correctly replace the noun 'one' is also the pronoun 'one' which means that the correct form of this statement is 'One should be sure not to forget one's kit tomorrow'. This sounds extremely stilted and awkward (and will become increasingly so in subsequent sentences) so, unless you are trying to create a particular effect in your writing, it's better to avoid using 'one' whenever possible.

Now let's consider this sentence:

● Leah was delighted to see her grandfather; she kissed him on the face.

In the second part of the sentence, it is clear who does the kissing and who receives the kiss as the two pronouns ('she' and 'him') are in the appropriate subject and object cases. As you can see, although the nouns ('Leah' and 'grandfather') do not change whether they are subject or object, their respective pronouns do. Similarly, pronouns change their form when they follow a preposition such as 'to'. For example:

● John had broken Leah's toy; he said sorry to her.

It would be incorrect to write *he said sorry to she*.

This situation, however, leads to another very common grammatical misunderstanding. Consider the following: your English teacher will certainly not approve if you begin a story with the words 'Me and my friends were going downtown' as we all know that the correct expression is 'My friends and I ...'. However, it is important that you don't let this format cloud your use of pronouns. The following sentence 'Lee apologised to my friend and I' is incorrect as it should be 'Lee apologised to my friend and me'. (If you find this confusing, think of the sentence 'Lee apologised to they', which is clearly wrong, as the object form of the pronoun, 'us', should be used.) It is important that you are always aware whether a pronoun is functioning as the subject or object in a sentence and give it the correct form.

Avoid possible confusions

Finally, here are two more areas of confusion. 'Who' is the subject case of the pronoun and 'whom' is the object. It can sometimes be very difficult to decide which one of the two should be used. For example, is it correct to say 'Who are you asking to the dance?' or 'Whom are you asking to the dance?' If you are in doubt, it will help to recast the sentence in your mind: 'I am asking he' or 'I am asking him'; the latter using the object pronoun 'him' is clearly correct and so it is correct to use 'whom' in the original sentence. Similarly, in the following choice 'Who/whom is your favourite teacher?' Recasting the sentence 'She is my favourite teacher' makes it clear that in this case you should use the subject case 'who'.

It is particularly important that you try to avoid any confusion of meaning or ambiguity when using pronouns. Consider the following statement:

- Maria likes Yousry more than me.
  The writer of this sentence presumably means

- Maria likes Yousry more than *she likes* me.
  but a reader might understand it as

- Maria likes Yousry more than *I do*.

The only way to avoid a common confusion of this sort is to ensure that you include words such as those in italics to make your meaning clear. Whatever you are writing, always try to keep in mind how your readers may interpret your words.

Exercise

Now read the following sentences carefully and correct all pronoun errors that they contain.

1 None of the boys was able to complete their assignments by the due date.
2 No-one has convincingly given their reason for not doing so.
3 The association will begin making plans for its meetings next month.
4 Neither of the teachers wanted to give their pupils punishments for being late to lessons.
5 Each of the schools told their pupils to go home early on Friday.
6 Although I studied economics when I was at school, I've forgotten everything I learned about them.
7 Every visitor to the theme park should be aware of the dangers they face.
8 If one knew what the most dangerous ride was, I would avoid it.
9 Neither of the boys remembered to bring their sports kit.
10 Both my sister and me love poetry but she likes it more than me.

Misplaced modifiers and dangling participles

Modifiers are words, phrases or clauses that add description and detail to sentences. They include adjectives, adverbs, phrases and clauses acting as adjectives or adverbs and phrases or clauses introduced by participles or prepositions.

Remember that modifying clauses and phrases, especially those introduced by participles, must be placed next to the word or words that they are describing; carelessness in placing modifiers can lead to your saying something rather different from that which you originally intended. The following sentence is an example:

- Piled up in an untidy heap on the ground, I started to burn the garden weeds.

In this sentence, the modifying clause at the beginning grammatically relates to the pronoun 'I' and suggests that the speaker has collapsed at the thought of the task he is about to begin! However, with a little alteration, the intended meaning can be made clear:

- I started to burn the garden weeds, piled up in an untidy heap on the ground.

However, it's not just groups of words that can cause problems; apparently simple and harmless single words can also seriously alter the meaning of a sentence if you are not careful about placing them precisely. Consider these two pairs of sentences and their exact meanings:

- Joe ate only porridge for breakfast.
- Joe ate porridge only for breakfast.

- I almost stayed awake for the whole concert.
- I stayed awake for almost the whole concert.

Remember, these may seem like trivial differences but they can seriously confuse a reader who may not be aware of your intended meaning.

Exercise

Explain carefully the difference in meaning in the following pairs of sentences and say which contains the writer's intended meaning.

a) While Joe was cooking the dinner, the dog chased the cat.
b) While cooking the dinner, the dog chased the cat.

c) Looking out of the window, the trees were swaying in the wind.
d) Standing on the balcony, we could see the trees swaying in the wind.

e) As I was walking across the road, a car splashed me with water.
f) Walking across the road, a car splashed me with water.

g) He was staring at the girl wearing a red dress at the bus stop.
h) He was staring at the girl at the bus stop wearing a red dress.

i) He nearly lost his footing walking across the stepping stones.
j) He lost his footing nearly walking across the stepping stones.

● Idiomatic expressions

English, like most other languages, contains many expressions which have a particular meaning to native speakers but which are almost nonsensical if taken literally or if translated directly into another language. These are known as idiomatic expressions and, in order to speak and write English convincingly, it is necessary to be familiar with them. By their very nature, idioms are going in and out of fashion and they also vary from one part of the world to another. In many cases their origin has become obscure or forgotten. For example, it is quite common to refer to someone whose behaviour is dangerous, because it is unpredictable and irresponsible, as 'a loose cannon'. However, very few people now realise that this phrase derives from the very real danger caused to sailors in earlier times by a cannon on a sailing warship that had broken loose from its fastenings and was rolling around uncontrollably as the ship pitched and tossed on the high seas.

It is not possible to give an exhaustive list of English idioms here, but the ones that are contained in the exercise below should give a flavour of the idiomatic expressions which are in use in everyday English.

A word of warning – some idiomatic expressions very quickly become unfashionable or turn into clichés; many of those contained in textbooks written many years ago will almost certainly not be in common use now. For example, it is now almost unheard of for an English teenager to ask a friend if he or she is 'in the pink of health', although in textbooks written in the days of your grandparents it would seem that nobody ever asked anything else! It is, of course, equally likely that future generations will no longer use many of the expressions in the following exercise.

Exercise

Match the idiomatic expression on the left with the correct definition on the right and then use each one in sentences of your own to show your understanding.

Expression	Definition
A feather in your cap	To have similar tastes and ideas to someone else
Fly off the handle	A person who is good-natured but who lacks polished manners and/or education
Mind their own business	A success that it is not likely to be repeated
Birds of a feather	To have done something to be proud of
Let the cat out of the bag	To spoil a person's chance of success
Like a dog with two tails	To deliberately ignore someone
A couch potato	To be very angry about something
Long in the tooth	People who are very similar in many ways
Rough diamond	Telling people not to interfere in something that does not concern them
A wet blanket	Saying someone looks completely innocent, but is capable of doing unpleasant things
Go the extra mile	To describe someone doing the wrong thing, out of incorrect or mistaken ideas or beliefs
Butter wouldn't melt in your mouth	Someone who spends a lot of time sitting and watching television
Pull a fast one	To do more than what is expected of you
Bark up the wrong tree	To be extremely happy
Tighten your belt	To be so unenthusiastic as to prevent other people from enjoying themselves
Give someone the cold shoulder	To make someone feel less confident, by doing or saying something that is unexpected
Speak the same language	To spend your money carefully
Take the wind out of someone's sails	To reveal a secret, often without meaning to
Cook somebody's goose	Someone who is a bit too old to do something
A flash in the pan	To gain an advantage over people by deceiving them

● Further spelling and vocabulary practice

As discussed previously, some English words are spelt differently depending upon what part of speech they are. Here are some examples.

Verb	Noun
advise	advice
affect	effect
license	licence
practise	practice
prophesy	prophecy

Exercise 1

Write sentences of your own containing each of the words in the list above to show the difference in their meanings and use.
   Note: 'Effect' can also be used as a verb; check its meaning by using a dictionary and then use it in a further sentence.

Exercise 2

There are many commonly used words in English that sound similar (even though they have completely different meanings) and whose meaning and spelling are easily confused. There are no easy rules for telling the difference, but it is important that you use them correctly in your writing in order to show your command of the language to the examiner who is marking your work. The most frequently used words are listed below. Check their meanings and spellings carefully and then ensure that you are able to use them confidently in sentences of your own. Don't try to do them all at once but make sure that you consolidate your awareness of them throughout the course.

accept/except/expect	allay/alley/ally
a lot/allot (**Note:** There is no such word as 'alot'!)	ascent/assent
allusion/illusion	altar/alter
bare/bear	capital/capitol
canvas/canvass	cite/sight/site
coarse/course	complement/compliment
consul/council/counsel	decent/descent/dissent
farther/further	formally/formerly
forth/fourth	hear/here
holy/wholly	isle/aisle

later/latter	lead/led
lessen/lesson	lose/loose
past/passed	peace/piece
personal/personnel	plain/plane
precedent/president	principal/principle
quiet/quite	rain/reign/rein
right/rite/write	stationary/stationery
statue/statute	then/than
there/their/they're	to/too/two
waive/wave	weak/week
wear/were/where	weather/whether
whole/hole	who's/whose
your/you're	

● Error recognition

Exercise

The following sentences all contain errors of some kind (mainly of usage, vocabulary or punctuation). Work through them and rewrite them, correcting all the errors you can find.

Note: Some of the sentences contain more than one error and there may be more than one way of correcting some of them.

1 He was feeling very boring and decided that he should hold a party for his friends'.
2 Here is the books that you borrowed from me last week.
3 Me and my friend was hurrying to school when she tripped and fell.
4 Although he was hungry, but he still didn't eat his supper as he didn't like it.
5 She ran to help her friend who fall off the swing.
6 'It wasn't I what done it, it was Daniel,' He shouted angrilly.
7 He inferred to me that Daniel was the culprit
8 I asked Jane to give the present to Jenny and I.
9 This is a nearly unique item.
10 The teacher collected the childrens' books altogether.
11 When I was buying some pens in the stationary shop, the assistant complemented me on my good taste.
12 Diving into the fast-flowing river the girl's hat was rescued by her boyfriend.
13 Don't kill yourself with work, let a computer do it!
14 I think it would be more better if we went on holiday next week.
15 Any of these two cars would be a good choice for a new driver.
16 This is the correct answer of the question.
17 He had barely chased the thief for twenty metres before he caught him.
18 My father is the coach of our football team, he also works in a bank.
19 Who's bicycle is that leaning against the fence?
20 In the boy's 100 metre heat, nobody managed to breach the qualifying time accept Kenneth.

Index

A
advertisements 26–9
apostrophes 126–7
assessment 2, 78–9, 111–19

B
booking forms 56–8
brochures 22–5

C
colons 106, 125
commas 106, 124
comprehension 2–3
coursework 119–21

D
dashes 127–8
direct speech: punctuation in 106, 128–9

E
error recognition 143
exclamation marks 106

F
facts 9–10, 11
factual texts 17–38
fiction 59–62, 99–100
form-filling 53–8
full stops 106

H
homographs 130
homonyms 130
homophones 130
hyphens 127–8

I
idioms 140–1
imaginative writing 59–62, 95–100
improving your writing 104–10
inferential questions 14

information transfer 53–8
informative writing 10–11, 17–38, 79–83

J
job applications 54–5

I
language control/choice 109
leaflets 17–22, 57
letters 91–5
listening coursework 120
listening skills 111
listening test 112–14
lists 103

M
manuals 35–6
modifiers 139–40

N
newspaper articles 40–5
note making 39–52

O
online guides 37–8, 47, 48–9
opinions 11

P
paragraphs 10, 107, 122–3
persuasive writing 83–91
planning your writing 101–3
pronouns 133–9
punctuation 106–7, 124–9

Q
question marks 106
questions 9–10, 14–15
  key words, identification of 4–6
  short-answer questions 16–29

R
reading skills 1–13, 14–38
recipes 29–30

S
scanning 4, 7, 9
semi-colons 106, 125
sentences 122: see also topic sentences
skimming 4, 7, 9
speaking coursework 119–20
speaking skills 111, 114–21
speaking test 114–19
spelling 105, 131, 142–3
spider diagrams 101–3
Standard English 104
summary writing 63–77
  example question 67–9
  practical guidelines 63–6
  practice passages 70–7
  style 66–7
  summary types 63

T
tenses 109
topic sentences 3, 10, 32, 79, 107, 123

V
verbs 131–3
vocabulary 130–7, 142–3

W
websites 31–2, 33–5
writing skills 78–110

Acknowledgements

The publishers would like to thank the following for permission to reproduce copyright material:

Text credits
p.8 'The Eiffel Tower', online article, adapted from *www.technologystudent.com/struct1/eiffel1.htm*; **p.11** 'Pompeii exhibition opens at the National Museum of Singapore' from Archaeology News Network, Art Daily (18 October, 2010); **pp.12–13** from 'Golconda Fort: Hyderabad's time machine', online from *Times of India* (9 January, 2013); **p.21** Brian Ward, 'Noise' *The Environment and Health* (Franklin Watts, 1989) and Department of the Environment, Transport and the Regions (DETR); **pp.23–25** 'Snow World India', website information, adapted slightly from *www.snowworldindia.net*; **pp.26–28** 'Adopt a dolphin', website material, adapted, reproduced by permission of Whale & Dolphin Conservation (WDC) UK; **p.30** Nava Atlas, 'Curried Pasta with Cauliflower and Chickpeas', from *The Vegetarian Family Cookbook*, copyright © 2004 by Nava Atlas. Used by permission of Broadway Books, an imprint of the Crown Publishing Group, a division of Random House LLC. All rights reserved; **pp.31–32** 'The history of the doughnut/hamburger/pizza', from *http://library.thinkquest.org/05aug/00509*; **p.33** Arthur C. Clarke, *Voice Across the Sea* (Frederick Muller/Harper & Row, 1958), reproduced by permission of David Higham; **p.34** 'Goldilocks and the 3 planets', article from *http://unawe.org/kids/unawe1347*, reproduced by permission of Pedro Russo; **pp.37–38** 'Lost or stolen phone', online information from Ofcom, *http://consumers.ofcom.org.uk/2013/03/lost-or-stolen-phone*, © Ofcom copyright; **pp.40–41** Ian Burrell, 'Thank God…it's a miracle', the *Independent* (1998), www.independent.co.uk reproduced by permission of ESI Media; **pp.42–43** John Naish, 'I refuse to use a mobile phone and I'm all the happier for it', online article from *Daily Mail* (5 February, 2013), reproduced by permission of Solo Syndication; **pp.44–45** Tracy McVeigh, 'Britain's women footballers use social media to promote game ignored by press', the *Observer* (8 April, 2012) copyright Guardian News & Media, reproduced by permission of the publisher; **pp.46–47** Robert Ballard, *The Discovery of the Titanic* (Orion, 1995); **pp.48–49** 'Seasons, weather and climate in Norway' from *www.visitnorway.com/uk/About-Norway/Seasons-and-climate-in-Norway*; **pp.50–51** 'Visit to Efteling Theme Park', adapted, *http://www.indianmomsconnect.com/2013/01/02visit-it-to-efteling-theme-park/* (2 January, 2013), reproduced by permission of Vibha (Chatty Wren); **p.52** Sheryl Garratt, 'Cheesy…but charming', the *Guardian* (25 November, 2001) copyright Guardian News & Media Ltd 2001, reproduced by permission of the publisher; **pp.59–60** Robert Louis Stevenson, *Treasure Island* (1883); **pp.61–62** Eleanor Porter, *Pollyanna* (1913); **pp.68–69** Noisy neighbours, article from *Which?*, the copyright in the Material is owned by Which? Limited and has been reproduced in *Cambridge IGCSE English as a Second Language book with CD* with their kind permission. The material must not be reproduced in whole or in part without the written permission of Which? Limited; **p.70** Jennifer Rosenberg, 'The Channel Tunnel', adapted, *http://history1900s.about.com/od/1990s/qt/Channel-Tunnel-Opens.htm*; **pp.71–72** Guy Grieve, 'The day I survived a very grizzly bear attack' from *Daily Mail* (26 November, 2009), reproduced by permission of Solo Syndication; **pp.72–73** Tracy McVeigh, 'Britain's women footballers use social media to promote game ignored by press', the *Observer* (8 April, 2012) copyright Guardian News & Media, reproduced by permission of Guardian News & Media Ltd; **pp.73–74** Karina Wilson, 'Early advertising' from *http://www.mediaknowall.com/as_alevel/Advertising/advertising.php?pageID=history*; **p.75** Brian Ward, 'Noise' *The Environment and Health* (Franklin Watts, 1989) and Department of the Environment, Transport and the Regions (DETR); **pp.76–77** 'Protecting children from pool accidents', the *New Straits Times* (5 July, 1994), reproduced by permission of the New Straits Times Press (M) Bhd; **pp.80–81** 'Checking in at the airport', information from *www.klm.com/travel/us_en/plan_and_book/special_offers/flight_offers/index.htm?WT.mc_id=1585961|3070841|38604450|208937870|785210*; **pp.82–83** Twitter article from Tesco online magazine from *www.tescomagazine.com/living/technology/a-beginners-guide-to-twitter.html*; **pp.85–86** Online article about school uniforms from *www.forandagainst.com/Why_Should_Kids_Wear_School_Uniform*; **p.87** Jade's Blog, 'Should More be Done to Protect Endangered Animals & Species?' from *http://jade4402.edublogs.org/2013/03/27/should-more-be-done-to-protect-endangered-animals-species*; **p.88** 'Endangered Species: The Asiatic Lion Asiatic Lion Facts' Last Updated: January 1, 2006 Glenn, C. R. 2006. "Earth's Endangered Creatures – Asiatic

ACKNOWLEDGEMENTS

Lion Facts" (Online), Accessed 9/17/2013 from *http://earthsendangered.com/profile.asp?sp=239&ID=3*, reproduced by permission of C. Renee Glenn; **p.89** 'Critically endangered lion now found only in India' from *http://wwf.panda.org/about_our_earth/teacher_resources/best_place_species/current_top_10/asiatic_lion_cfm*, reproduced by permission of WWF; **p.90** 'Asian lion' from *http://animals.nationalgeographic.com/animals/mammals/asian-lion*, reproduced by permission of National Geographic Creative; **p.97** Flann O'Brien, extract from *The Third Policeman* (Harper Perennial Modern Classics, 2007); **p.98** Richard Hughes, extract from *A High Wind in Jamaica* (Vintage, 2002); **pp.99–100** Deb Brainard, 'There is a ghost in my closet' online short story from *www.storystar.com/php/read_story.php?story_id=1580*; **pp.108–109** David Jones, 'Murderball', *Daily Mail* (5 September, 2012), reproduced by permission of Solo Syndication

Section 1 on the CD

pp.1–2 'Healthy eating for teens', article from *www.nhs.uk/Livewell/Goodfood/Pages/healthy-eating-teens.aspx*, © Crown copyright; **pp.3–4** 'Hurricanes', article from *www.weatherwizkids.com/weather-hurricane.htm*; **pp.5–6** Simon Smith, 'Behind the timetable: a day in the life of an English teacher', article from *www.theguardian.com/teacher-network/teacher-blog/2013/jul/31/teacher-timetable-day-in-life-english-teacher*, copyright Guardian News & Media Ltd 2012, reproduced by permission of the publisher; **pp.13–14** Waheeda Harris, 'Exploring Northern Peru – the alluring Amazon rainforest' from *http://o.canada.com/travel/exploring-northern-peru-the-alluring-amazon-rainforest/* (September 3, 2013), © Postmedia News; **p.15** Fred Mawer, 'Parc Asterix: leave the queues and hype behind', article from *www.telegraph.co.uk/travel/familyholidays/7851148/Parc-Asterix-leave-the-queues-and-hype-behind.html*, reproduced by permission of Telegraph Media Group; **p.16** 'An Introduction to Sea Turtles', from *www.conserveturtles.org/seaturtleinformation.php?page=overview*, reproduced by permission of Sea Turtle Conservancy, www.conserveturtles.org

Audio on the CD

Track 5 Mary Bagley, 'Mount Vesuvius & Pompeii: Facts & History' from *www.livescience.com/27871-mount-vesuvius-pompeii.html*, reproduced by permission of Wright's Media; **Track 6** 'Beekeeping', adapted from *www.hobbyfarms.com/crops-and-gardening/beekeeping-14945.aspx* (i-5Publishing LLC)

Permission for re-use of all © Crown copyright information is granted under the terms of the Open Government Licence (OGL).

Photo credits

p.1 *t* © Photos.com/Getty Images/Thinkstock, *b* © Getty Images/iStockphoto/Thinkstock; **p.2** ©Andy Chang – Fotolia; **p.5** © Getty Images/Jupiterimages/Thinkstock; **p.8** ©Andrew Ward/Life File/Photodisc/Getty Images; **p.12** ©BasPhoto – Fotolia; **p.23** © http://commons.wikimedia.org/wiki/File:India_-_Hyderabad_-_061_-_Snow_World_%283920051021%29.jpg/http://creativecommons.org/licenses/by/2.0/deed.en; **p.27** © WDC/Charlie Phillips; **p.28** © WDC/Charlie Phillips; **p.32** © Erwin Purnomosidi/Getty Images/Hemera/Thinkstock; **p.34** *t* ©ESO/M. Kornmesser/http://creativecommons.org/licenses/by/3.0/, *b* ©ESO/UNAWE; **p.45** © Joern Pollex/Getty Images; **p.40** © Ralph White/Corbis; **p.50** © Efteling bv; **p.51** © Efteling bv; **p.54** © blackdovfx/Getty Images/iStockphoto/Thinkstock; **p.57** ©M_a_y_a/Getty Images/iStockphoto/Thinkstock; **p.70** Herbert Ortner/http://commons.wikimedia.org/wiki/File:Eurostar_3012_Waterloo.jpg/http://creativecommons.org/licenses/by/3.0/deed.en; **p.71** © lightplay – Fotolia; **p.76** © Patrik Giardino/Corbis; **p.82** © Robert Kneschke – Fotolia; **p.85** © michaeljung – Fotolia; **p.88** © Mukesh Acharya – Fotolia; **p.90** © Dyan_k/Getty Images/iStockphoto/Thinkstock; **p.108** © Mark Davidson/Alamy

t = top, *b* = bottom

Every effort has been made to trace all copyright holders, but if any have been inadvertently overlooked the publishers will be pleased to make the necessary arrangements at the first opportunity.